CUSTOMER EXPERIENCE MANAGEMENT

A revolutionary approach to
connecting with your customers

BERND H. SCHMITT

Author of **EXPERIENTIAL MARKETING**

JOHN WILEY & SONS, INC.

To the late Bill Brandt
For his kindness, support, and humanity

PREFACE

Customer *Experience Management,* or CEM, is, I admit, a sequel. It is a sequel to my best-selling book, *Experiential Marketing,* that has been translated into more than 10 languages. *Experiential Marketing* offered a new marketing paradigm that argues for a customer-focused instead of a product- or brand-focused approach and shows how managers can create a variety of experiences (*sense, feel, think, act,* and *relate*) for their customers. *Customer Experience Management* is the next step providing a powerful framework for managing the customer experience step-by-step in a strategic and creative way. Key concepts from the first book will be summarized here; however, the overlap is less than 10 percent.

This sequel was necessary for several reasons. First, managers who had read *Experiential Marketing* confessed to me that even though they admired the approach, they were not always sure how to manage an "experience project." That became the basis for this book: a straightforward, five-step process for managing your customer's experience, outlined in Chapter 2 and then discussed step-by-step with corresponding methodologies in Chapters 3 through 7.

Second, when I wrote *Experiential Marketing*, "experience" was a new term. Now, the situation is quite different. Through my book and other works (e.g., Lou Carbone's work on customer-centric service, Jerry Zaltman's work on Z-met, Pine and Gilmore's book on the experience economy, Patricia Seybold's book on the customer revolution, Shaun Smith's work in the United Kingdom on "experiencing the brand," and Gerhard Schulze's research in Germany on the experience society) experience is now a word in every manager's vocabulary. Managers are beginning to understand the importance of focusing on the customer experience and doing so in an integrative fashion. This book is designed to show managers how to use the power of an experiential approach to connect with the customer at every touchpoint. For the first time, managers can learn how to deliver a seamlessly integrated customer experience (see Chapter 8, on integration).

Moreover, managers are increasingly asked to justify financial investments. That is, they need to build a model that would link experience to tangible outcomes. The focus of CEM is on enhancing customer value through managing the customer experience, and Chapter 9 provides you with a model that links the customer experience to "customer equity."

Finally, to practice CEM successfully, managers need not only a framework, methodologies, and models but also up-to-date business cases that can serve as benchmarks. Over the last five years, as a consultant and as CEO of The EX Group, I have consulted and developed brand and experience strategies for clients in consumer package goods, automobile, electronics, software, financial services, pharmaceuticals, beauty and cosmetics, hospitality, and media industries. In this book, I will share with you some of these cases and describe many others that you can use as benchmarks for successful customer experience management.

Enjoy the reading experience!

ACKNOWLEDGMENTS

Many people have supported me in writing this book. Nick Peterson has been involved in many aspects of this project: he researched cases, secured permissions, provided the key liaison with my publisher, and has contributed original photos and photo collages. Special thanks go to Laura Brown, my colleague Professor Sunil Gupta, Claudia Laviada, Dave Myers, David Rogers, David Sussman, and especially Airie Stuart, my inspiring editor at John Wiley & Sons. All of you have transformed the laborious process of writing this book into a personally enriching and rewarding experience.

I dedicate this book to Bill Brandt, a former professor at Columbia Business School and co-founder of Impact Planning Group. Bill passed away during the time I was writing this book. He was loved by everyone for his kindness, support, and professionalism. He left an immense legacy, having consulted with more than 400 corporations worldwide on how to become customer oriented, market focused, and externally oriented. He supported me as a mentor and teacher in a manner that was truly extraordinary in its dedication and humanity.

CONTENTS

Contents

CHAPTER

1

Taking the Customer
Seriously—Finally

C
ompanies of all kinds acknowledge that their customers
are important; that customers are the company's most
valuable asset; that the company survives only when it
has customers and grows only when it can retain them and recruit new ones; and that the company, therefore, should be
structured and managed around the customer.

You have heard such proclamations many times—in CEO
speeches, in press releases, and in the phone queue waiting for
a customer service representative. In a survey that I conducted
in 2002 at Columbia Business School with more than a hun-
dred U.S. managers, *customer focus* was identified as the single
most important differentiator between the best and worst
companies in an industry.

But what about customers' actual experiences? How are customers really being treated? The answer is "badly," despite all the protestations to the contrary. Customers are still being treated as if they didn't matter or as if they were an afterthought to the company's really important concerns. Take a look at these situations:

- You are a loyal and valuable airline customer. You spend more than 70 days per year up in the skies, usually in international travel, in first or business class on 747s. You are now about to cash in on the rewards of your loyalty: You are booking a vacation for you and your family with those carefully accumulated frequent flyer miles. How does your favorite airline treat you now? Is your trip an occasion for the airline to celebrate your loyalty? Are you a key priority, a valuable asset on that "special ticket"? Not likely. For many airlines, you are the lowest priority because you are not a revenue-generating passenger on that particular trip. You are a sucker, a parasite. And you will be treated accordingly: filling out forms to get the ticket, waiting on low-priority reservation lines, paying extra to get your tickets delivered. You are not eligible for upgrades. You get lowest priority on standby lists. If anything goes wrong during the trip—such as a cancellation due to bad weather or problems with the aircraft—you are the last to be informed and the last to have your problems resolved. So much for being a loyal, valuable customer all those years.
- You go to a local fast-food restaurant. The restaurant is dirty. The restrooms are filthy. The whole place smells of

grease. The service people behind the counter manage to take your order, give you change, and fill up your tray without looking at you once. The seats are screwed into the walls so far from the tables that you can barely reach your food. Sure, the food was cheap—but do you deserve this kind of treatment?

- You hear about a new online pet-food store and think, hey, that would be better than dragging home 40-pound bags of dog chow. You get onto the site, find your way around it— which is not easy—and manage to checkout using your credit card. At 7:30 the next morning, you get a call from a customer service representative who says their e-commerce software has "failed to capture" your credit card information and could you please give it to her again. She's "pretty sure" they have the rest of the order information correct. In the cold light of morning, you think twice about entrusting your credit card information to a company with such unreliable software, and you tell the caller to cancel the order. The next day you get another call from a different customer service person, asking you again for your credit card information. You repeat your cancellation. Two days later, it happens again, and not one of these three customer service people realizes that either of the others has called. You finally manage to cancel the order, but you still cannot get off their newsletter e-mailing list because the "unsubscribe" function doesn't work.

- You run your own business, a management consulting firm, but it is difficult to do business with most of your vendors (IT service providers, graphic design firms, messenger services, etc.). In this age of the Internet, you still have to pick up the phone and fill out paper invoices to order their goods and services. Some of the vendors keep you on a phone line waiting for service for extended periods. Some vendors cannot e-mail order confirmations. Can't these suppliers improve the way they serve your business?

All of these bad experiences—and many, many more—have happened to me over the course of writing this book. I am the guy who buys the yogurt with the bad packaging and spills it all over his suit. I am the one waiting 25 minutes on hold for customer service or standing around at the counter while the salesperson chats on the phone. I am the guy under the desk trying to connect the peripheral device in a forest of cords that all look exactly alike.

Unless I am particularly unlucky, you probably have similar stories to report. If you browse any of the complaint Web sites on the Internet, you will find thousands of such stories from dissatisfied customers.

The bad treatment many customers receive is not just a matter of the incidental failure of a particular aspect of customer management. It is not just that the Web site is poorly set up, or that the person at the call center had a bad day, or that this particular model of the product has a glitch. These failures are symptomatic of broader problems in the organization. Despite their insistence about the key importance of the customer, many companies are still systematically failing to provide their customers with positive experiences.

In fact, the problem is not just with a few companies here and there; entire industries seem to have caught the disease of

FIGURE 1.1

Frustrating customer situations: opening a badly designed yogurt container, waiting on the phone for customer service, connecting computer peripherals, trying to open alarm clock packaging. *Credit:* Photos by Nick Peterson.

customer mismanagement and abuse: car dealers, insurance companies, and electronics retailers are on the list of customer abusers for many people. Life as a customer can be really tough; sometimes it may seem as if you just have to live with inferior goods and poor service: *C'est la vie!*

But wait. Even in the most customer-unfriendly industries, I can usually find at least one good—if not splendid—company that exemplifies the provision of outstanding customer experiences. Poor treatment of customers does not have to be a way of life. The examples discussed next come from the same industries as those presented earlier, but they illustrate very different treatment of customers:

- Singapore Airlines focuses on delivering an extraordinary experience—"a great way to fly"—through outstanding service. In its annual report, the company states: "Our aim is to provide the highest standards of service in the aviation industry"; it focuses on "all aspects of the travel experience in whatever class of service." In the course of my consulting and speaking engagements, I have spoken with hundreds of executives who have flown Singapore Airlines and almost all of them have been full of praise. The company has thought through every step of the customer experience, even in economy class: a friendly and competent reservation agent serves customers making reservations; the check-in procedure is fast and efficient; a flight attendant with a warm and natural smile greets passengers entering the plane; one of the attendants walks each passenger to his or her seat; at the seat, there is an amenities box; during the trip, the flight attendants are attentive; and so on and on. You can only imagine what executives report about business and first class. This airline has been an innovator in managing their customers' experience over the years: They were the first to have sleeper seats, dozens of channels in economy class, Internet booking for international reservations, and many other breakthroughs.

- For a great fast-food experience, go to Starbucks. Of course, it's not called "fast food." In fact, the service may even be a little slow. That is all part of the experience. There is much more to feel and experience in Starbucks than in the typical fast-food dump. This "Third Space" between home and office, as the company's CEO has described its positioning platform, strives to provide an outstanding customer experience.

- How about online ordering? In contrast to my bad experience with the pet-food site, Amazon.com provides a marvelous online shopping experience. The site has the right look and feel, as well as an amazing interface. What is more, Amazon.com is continuously improving on the experience. We will take a closer look at this successful and innovative company in Chapter 7.

- For sending packages and other shipments from business to business, Federal Express (FedEx) has developed convenient Web-based shipping tools that get the job done fast and easily via the Internet right from your desktop. Or you can also give your front office employees the power to ship, track, and handle reports from their personal computers (PCs). There is more: Through FedEx, you can buy or lease a PC, handle all invoicing electronically, and track the shipment at any time.

FIGURE 1.2

Delightful customer situations: playing cards from Singapore Airlines, enjoying a Starbucks coffee, cruising on a Razor Scooter, relaxing with a cucumber eye mask. *Credit:* Photos by Nick Peterson.

There is hope for better customer experiences. The companies in these counterexamples achieved extraordinary customer care. I featured some of these companies in my earlier book *Experiential Marketing*, and I provide many more outstanding examples throughout this book. These companies serve as benchmarks for a successful focus on the customer experience.

If all of this sounds supremely sensible, why are most companies doing such a bad job? If Singapore Airlines, Starbucks, Amazon.com, Federal Express, and others can succeed, why can't more companies take the customer experience more seriously? And why, despite all their public declarations, are most companies still unable to treat customers the way they deserve to be treated? Are these companies just cynical? Is all that "your call is important to us" and "be assured your business is of great value to us" just marketing talk?

Occasionally, perhaps, but not for the large majority of cases. The problem is that such companies have been relying on outdated and misguided marketing and management approaches that present themselves as customer-focused but fail to help companies connect with their customers.

Three Misguided Approaches: The Marketing Concept, Customer Satisfaction, and CRM

What approaches am I referring to? Many of the companies that talk about the importance of the customer rely on one of three paradigms: the "marketing concept," "customer satisfaction," or "customer relationship management." In the following sections, I describe these paradigms and explain why I call them "the devil in disguise."

The Marketing Concept

In the 1990s, companies increasingly acknowledged the critical importance of becoming "customer-oriented" and "market-driven" instead of product-, technology-, or sales-focused. Becoming customer-oriented and market-driven is the core of what marketing scholars have called the *marketing concept.* This is how Philip Kotler, a well-known marketing author, summarizes the marketing concept:

> The *marketing concept* holds that the key to achieving organizational goals consists of determining the needs and wants of target markets and delivering the desired satisfactions more effectively and efficiently than competitors. It starts with a well-defined market, focuses on customer needs, coordinates all the activities that will affect customers, and produces profits by satisfying customers.[1]

"Determining the needs and wants of target markets," "delivering the desired satisfactions," "focuses on customer needs," "coordinates all the activities that will affect customers"—it all sounds good, doesn't it?

In fact, marketers have even developed a formal measure of the degree to which companies live the marketing concept. It is called the *market orientation scale.* The scale consists of 20 items that companies can use to diagnose the degree to which they are customer- and market-focused. The scale includes three sub-components that form the backbone of the marketing concept:

1. *Intelligence generation.* The collection of information about customer needs and competition through market research.

10

2. *Intelligence dissemination.* The spreading of the collected information cross-functionally and organization-wide.

3. *Responsiveness.* Acting on the collected information to satisfy customers (e.g., by incorporating customer intelligence into new product development).

When managers take a close look at the concepts, models, and tools of the traditional marketing field, they soon realize that traditional marketing is not at all customer-oriented. As I showed in *Experiential Marketing,* the field of marketing is fundamentally engineering- and logistics-driven; instead of focusing on the customer, marketing remains product-focused and sales-oriented:

- Most concepts and tools focus narrowly on functional features and benefits of products; traditional marketing lacks concepts that can account for the image and imaginative qualities that a product may provide.

- Markets and competition are defined on the basis of similarities in features and benefits; as a result, a broader and more appropriate view of markets and competition (based on consumption and usage situations) is missing.

- Customers are seen simply as rational decision makers who trade off functional features and benefits in their minds, when in fact they frequently engage in emotion-, intuition-, and impulse-driven purchases.

- Market research is a purely analytical and a mostly verbal undertaking, and methods that study customers in their natural environments are seen as unreliable and invalid.

11

- Marketing strategy's holy cow is "differentiation," another product-focused concept. Differentiation of a consumer product does not guarantee that the product is relevant to a consumer's life. Differentiation of an industrial good does not guarantee the good solves a business customer's problems. Differentiation is just that—being different—and often in trivial aspects that are irrelevant to the customer.

- Marketing implementations through the Four P's (product, price, promotion, and place) consist of a product-centered "to-do list" that specifies that the product needs to be packaged, priced, advertised, and distributed; but where is the "C" (the customer) in the Four P's? How many product design, pricing, promotion, and distribution decisions actually focus on the customer?

- The marketing orientation scale is information-focused and quite generic. It can be useful as a broad assessment tool, but not for strategizing or planning a customer-oriented initiative. Empirically, the scale is only weakly correlated with organizational success. What is most confusing about the marketing concept is that it presents product-focused concepts and methods in the guise of a customer-oriented approach. As a result, if you rely exclusively on this concept and its methodologies, you are unlikely to fully understand your customers.

Customer Satisfaction

Another approach that presents itself as customer-focused—but isn't—is *customer satisfaction*. We all believe that customer satisfaction creates customer loyalty; therefore, the objective of this approach is to ensure that customers are satisfied after they have purchased a product or otherwise interacted with the company.

When are customers actually satisfied? According to this model, satisfaction is an outcome-oriented attitude deriving from customers who compare the performance of the product with their expectations of it. If the product is below customers' expectations, they will be dissatisfied; if it is above expectations, customers will be satisfied.

Here we go again. In the customer satisfaction framework, expectations and performance are viewed in purely functional, product-driven terms. What does the customer expect in terms of product functions? What does he or she expect to get out of the product? How did the performance of the product (e.g., its quality) stack up?

What is absent from this approach is a consideration of all the experiential dimensions of product consumption that matter to customers. These dimensions may include how the product (or service) makes customers feel, what emotional associations they may have with it, and how the product or service may help customers relate to other people or groups of people. A whole world of experiential connections is waiting to be explored, and traditional customer satisfaction fails to take us anywhere near it.

The satisfaction paradigm has been used widely in the automotive industry, which has developed detailed functional measures of cars to track customer satisfaction. This industry illustrates the paradigm's shortcomings. Being satisfied with a car is more than having an engine that runs smoothly. On functional attributes, many cars are equal. As important, if not more so, are styling, aesthetics, entertainment features, lifestyle considerations, and prestige—all aspects of driving and owning a car that rarely appear in satisfaction surveys.

Moreover, given the neat "Satisfaction = Loyalty" equation that the customer satisfaction paradigm is built on, most satisfaction measures have been bad predictors of customer loyalty. So, once again, something has to be missing.

Ironically, the customer is what is missing. Like the marketing concept, the customer satisfaction model is far more concerned with the functionality of the product than with the experience of the customer.

I expect some of you are saying, "Isn't customer experience just a fancy word for customer satisfaction?" Not really. Think about it this way: Suppose you were to ask your partner two questions after sex: "Were you satisfied?" and "How was the experience?" I predict you might get very different answers to these two questions. (You might also get different kinds of answers from men and women, but let's leave that aside.) The concept of satisfaction is outcome-oriented. Were you satisfied with shopping? "Sure I got what I wanted." Are you satisfied with your car? "Yes, it drives well." "Were you satisfied with sex?" (You fill in the blank.)

Experience, in contrast, is process-oriented. The shopping experience includes much more than simply getting what you want. It focuses on all the events and activities that were part of it: the design of the shopping environment in the store or online, the service personnel, how they greeted you, whether you bought something extra, and how you felt while you were shopping. The same for the car experience: the way the door sounds when you close it, the way the fabric feels, how the dealer treats you. For sex? All those sensory, affective, intellectual, and bodily stimulations (to put it scientifically). . . . So how does the leading condom brand position itself? "Trojan—for the most enjoyable experience."

Now ask yourself as a manager, which idea—satisfaction or experience—provides more guidance for adding value to customers. Clearly, experience provides much more guidance because it forces you to identify the details that result in satisfaction. If you go through the process of managing the customer experience, satisfaction is likely to be one of the results. But experience is what you need to understand and manage. If you pay attention to the experience, satisfaction occurs naturally. As an added bonus, experience—far more than satisfaction alone—will differentiate your company in the eyes of your customers. Providing powerful and compelling customer experiences will set you apart from your competitors in a way that focusing on simple satisfaction never will.

Customer Relationship Management

A recent entrant to the arena of so-called customer-oriented approaches is customer relationship management (CRM).

Customer relationship management means different things to different people: it may refer to direct mail, mass customization, databases that do online analytical processing (OLAP), or customer interaction centers (CICs). In practical terms, however, CRM consists primarily of databases and software programs used in call centers. Software applications of CRM have become a huge business, just as reengineering and total quality management (TQM) were in the late 1980s and 1990s.

However, even after running $50-million CRM programs over three to five years, companies are often dissatisfied and feel that their results lack differentiation and customer focus.

This disappointment occurs because, despite the *relationship* in its name, CRM focuses on transactions, not on building relationships. Companies record in data fields only what is easy to measure and record, not the less quantifiable information that could complete the picture of the customer. Even with enormous computing power, the data collected are often purely recordings of monetary transactions and operations (e.g., when the customer bought what where; when the salespeople showed up; what piece of equipment was exchanged; when the customer checked into a hotel; and how much he or she spent in which restaurant outlet).

The problem with CRM is that it focuses on information that is important to the company and occasionally helps to shape customer behavior through what is called *operant conditioning* (the consequences of customers' spending patterns), but it rarely establishes an emotional bond with the customer. Other needs besides functional ones are neglected. Customer feedback is usually not included. Moreover, most CRM programs can be copied—all you need is the software, some integration with existing systems, and "deep pockets"—not easy requirements, but not prohibitive for most companies either.

Most important, building a relationship requires integration across a variety of touchpoints. But CRM databases are usually not integrated with brand-focused customer initiatives such as advertising, promotions, or special events. Despite its attractive title, then, customer relationship management does not manage relationships with customers.

The Need for a New Approach

The marketing concept, customer satisfaction, and customer relationship management all promise to help managers better understand their customers. However, each approach has remained narrowly focused and unnecessarily limiting. What's more, they often distract management from really focusing on the customer. That's why I call them "the devil in disguise."

What managers need is an approach that takes the customer seriously—finally. Such an approach would provide a view of the *total* customer experience. It would focus not only on functional product features and functional transactions but also on anything else that provides value during decision making, purchase, and usage. It would enable managers to create products and services that consistently delight customers and provide profits for the firm. This approach would define markets and competition based on broad sociocultural and business usage contexts, and companies would use this insight in new product development and deployment. Finally, it would use research to gather broad-based customer intelligence instead of precise but inconsequential measurements.

Customer experience management is that approach.

What Is Customer Experience Management?

To put it simply, customer experience management (CEM) is the process of strategically managing a customer's entire experience with a product or a company.

As you will see in this book, CEM is a truly customer-focused management concept (not a "marketing" concept).

It is a process-oriented satisfaction idea (not an outcome-oriented one). In addition, CEM goes far beyond CRM by moving from recording transactions to building rich relations with customers.

CEM has a broad view of how a company and its products can be relevant to a customer's life. CEM connects with the customer at every touchpoint and calls for the integration of different elements of the customer's experience. It recognizes that customers don't buy a car just because it operates well and a computer just because it has sufficient storage, memory, and plug-ins. A car is also an identity-projecting lifestyle product, and it is as important for a computer to spark the imagination as to store data. CEM is concerned with sales and brand preference, but that is not the whole story. Before and even after the sale, CEM provides value to customers by delivering information, service, and interactions that result in compelling experiences. It thus builds loyalty with customers and adds value to the firm.

CEM also takes an integrative approach to the organization, looking internally as well as externally. A manifestation of this integration is its attention to the employee experience because employees influence customers' perceptions of the company. Therefore, to create a delightful customer experience, employees must be motivated, competent at their jobs, and innovative in their thinking. To do all this, employees need to have the right experience with the company they work for. Managers cannot just impose initiatives from the top down; these initiatives have to be an integral part of the whole organization. This point is most obvious with services, but the principle applies to any business. To deliver the right look and feel and the right

---

Box 1.1

DOES CUSTOMER EXPERIENCE HAVE MEASURABLE EFFECTS?

Several empirical studies have addressed this question. In 2001 and 2002, ADK, a communication firm, conducted an extensive series of studies in which more than 1,000 male and female customers ranging from 20 to 49 years old participated.

Separate studies assessed the relationship between experience and advertising effectiveness between experience and store impact, and between experience and Web site effectiveness. The studies were conducted as mall intercepts and Internet surveys.

The research employed a revised and improved version of the EX Scale that I featured in *Experiential Marketing* as a measure of experiential value. To have a reliable and valid scale that could be used to measure experiential value for all sorts of stimuli (products, ads, stores, Web sites), the scale development itself included several thousand consumers. For the results reported here, the EX Scale values were correlated with customers' overall impressions, attitudes, and purchase intentions for dozens of TV ads, stores, and Web sites.

The following figure shows the statistical correlations between the value on the EX Scale and the impression, attitude, and purchase intention measures. Note that all correlations exceed a value of .4 and that two-thirds even exceed .7.

(continued)

19

Box 1.1   Continued

Correlations Between Experience and Customer Behavior

	Customer Impressions	Attitude	Purchase Intention
TV Ads	.51	.77	.59
Stores	.75	.74	.84
Web Sites	.81	.45	.76

These high numbers and strong relationships indicate that more experiential ads, stores, and Web sites result in higher impressions, more positive attitudes, and greater purchase intentions.

In addition, the next figure shows the relationship between GRPs (gross rating points), a measure of the total audience delivery, and awareness. In 12 out of the 13 cases used in this research, the awareness scores for the experiential ads were above the standard awareness curve. This strongly suggests that experiential communications draw greater attention and create stronger awareness and memory than other communications.

An experience project thus offers great value to a firm. Moreover, the costs of a CEM project usually do not exceed those of comparable marketing and management initiatives

---

Box 1.1 Continued

and are in fact often considerably lower, especially when the experience is an integrated one (see Chapter 8). As a result, the return on investment (ROI) of a CEM project usually exceeds those of other initiatives.

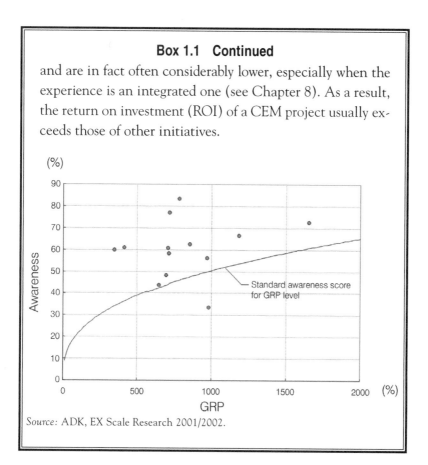

Source: ADK, EX Scale Research 2001/2002.

---

interaction, and to be innovative in the marketplace, employees need to focus not just on numbers and spreadsheets, but also on the customer experience.

Finally, CEM is not an amorphous business philosophy. It is a practical management tool that can show you in detail how you can provide experiential value to customers and, in turn, derive financial value for your firm.

Conclusion

CEM is a new paradigm that represents a radical break from the old marketing and management approaches. It offers analytical and creative insight into the customer's world, strategic tools for shaping that world, and implementation tools that companies can use to increase customer value. Chapter 2 describes the five-step CEM framework which you can use to connect with your customer and grow your business.

An Overview of the CEM Framework

My extensive work with companies has shown me the widespread, urgent need for a framework that focuses on the customer experience. The key to company growth and profitability can be summarized in a simple formula: analyze the customer experience, then develop an experience-focused strategy, and add value through integrated implementations that focus on the customer experience. This chapter outlines the five-step customer experience management (CEM) framework that delivers growth and profitability.

CEM Solves a Variety of Business Problems

The CEM framework solves a wide range of business problems. The following projects—some of which are described in detail in later chapters—are just a few of the CEM projects I have participated in over the past few years:

- A cosmetics company redesigning the customer experience for a leading brand whose sales had become stagnant.
- A pharmaceutical company adding interactivity with customers to its traditional R&D focus and making the experience (of both customers and employees) a key leadership initiative.
- A company in the information business reorganizing entirely around the customer experience.
- A nonprofit organization in the music business repositioning its brand and expanding the customer experience.
- A company in the beauty business launching a new brand with contemporary experiential appeal.
- An advertising agency developing planning tools and metrics to provide experiential communications for their customers.
- A company in the electronics business launching an experiential product.

Other businesses also have used the concepts and methodologies in this book to design experiential solutions for all sorts of situations. The projects ranged from the design of an experience for an Indonesian local airline to the in-store experience of a Swiss supermarket retailer to the South American market launch for a leading software product.

The CEM framework provides a powerful solution for business challenges in all kinds of industries. Throughout this book, there are examples of successful implementations of this framework.

Moreover, the CEM framework sheds new light on perennial marketing and management issues such as segmentation and targeting, positioning, branding, service, and innovation.

The Five Steps of the CEM Framework

The CEM framework has five basic steps (see Figure 2.1). As explained later in this chapter, managers have some flexibility in the order in which they carry out these steps. For now, I am presenting them in sequence.

Step 1: Analyzing the Experiential World of the Customer

The first step of the CEM framework provides original insight into the customer's world. For consumer markets, it is necessary

step 1   Analyzing the experiential world of the customer

step 2   Building the experiential platform

step 3   Designing the brand experience

step 4   Structuring the customer interface

step 5   Engaging in continuous innovation

FIGURE 2.1

The Five Steps of the CEM Framework

to analyze the sociocultural context in which consumers operate including their experiential needs and wants, as well as their lifestyles. For business-to-business (B2B) markets, we need to analyze the business context including requirements and solutions that might impact the experience of customers. Management must relate broad-based lifestyle and business trends to the usage situations and ultimately to the brand—a process that I refer to as "funneling."

Here is an example from my own consulting experience—a project for an international sparkling-wine maker. The wine industry worldwide is extremely product focused. The objective of this project was to differentiate the company not by product but by the customer experience, by focusing on the situations in which people enjoy drinking sparkling wine. I used the concepts and methodologies of this step to identify usage and consumption situations for drinking wine that could generate new revenues. The situations and pertinent experiences that reflected broader sociocultural trends included "spending a romantic evening with someone special," "rewarding yourself after you get home from work," and "treating yourself to some sparkle after the theater." Then I examined how various brands of the company would fit into these situations in a competitive context.

Chapter 3 provides a detailed discussion of how to analyze your customers' experiential world.

Step 2: Building the Experiential Platform

The experiential platform is the key connection point between strategy and implementation. It is not a cut-and-dried positioning statement or a two-dimensional perceptual map with generic verbal labels. Instead, the experiential platform includes a dynamic, multisensory, multidimensional depiction of the desired experience (referred to as "experiential positioning"). It also specifies the value that the customer can expect from the product (the "experiential value promise" or EVP). The platform culminates in an overall implementation theme for coordinating subsequent marketing and communication efforts and future innovation.

In one of my consulting projects, a vitamin manufacturer asked for an experiential platform that could pull together the entire product line with a common implementation theme. The selected theme focused on the concept of *vivere* (living life to its fullest) and how different vitamins provide different experiential benefits (sensory acumen, a positive mind, an energized body, etc.).

Chapter 4 explains how to build an experiential platform for your own company and brands.

Step 3: Designing the Brand Experience

After management has decided on the experiential platform, it must be implemented in the brand experience. Whether you are in a consumer or B2B market, the brand experience includes, first, experiential features and product aesthetics that can serve as a jumping-off point for the customer's brand experience. Next, the brand experience includes an appealing "look and feel" in logos and signage, packaging, and retail spaces. Finally, appropriate experiential messages and imagery in advertising and collaterals, as well as online, complete the brand experience.

In my own consulting, I have used the concepts and methodologies of this step in client projects for both launching new brands and repositioning existing ones. Designing the brand experience for new brands requires creativity to differentiate it in unusual ways in the marketplace. For existing brands, the task includes deciding which features, the look and feel, and what messages to keep, drop, change, or add. I refer to this procedure as "brand stripping and dressing." First, the brand is stripped of nonessential and inappropriate elements (e.g., a confusing name or logo, an ineffective ad campaign, an inappropriate store design). Then it is dressed up with new desirable elements (a new name, logo, ad campaign, store design).

Chapter 5 focuses on how to design the brand experience.

Step 4: Structuring the Customer Interface

The experiential platform must also be implemented in the customer interface. Whereas the brand experience is largely static (once designed, it remains much the same for some time), the customer interface is dynamic and interactive. Step 4 includes all sorts of dynamic exchanges and contact points with the customer—face-to-face in a store, during a sales visit in a client's office, at an automatic teller machine at a bank, at the check-in desk of a hotel, or as part of e-commerce on the Internet. It is important to structure the content and style of this dynamic interaction to give the customer the desired information and service in the right interactive manner. Structuring the customer interface goes beyond CRM, which merely records the history and transaction content of such contacts and provides informational links. The interface design must incorporate intangible elements (i.e., voice, attitude, and behavioral style) and address experiential consistency over time and coherence among various touchpoints.

Eli Lilly, the pharmaceutical company, had chosen a new brand identity and slogan for the new century: "Answers that Matter." The company soon realized that this message had to be more than just a new slogan: it also required a new interface with the customer and a new conception of how everyone in the organization would view their jobs and interact with customers. The result was an exciting new behavioral and human resources communication program that used some of the key concepts of the CEM framework.

In Chapter 6, there is detailed advice on structuring the customer interface.

Step 5: Engaging in Continuous Innovation

Finally, the company's innovations must reflect the experiential platform—a process I call "engaging in continuous innovation." Innovations include anything that improves end customers' personal lives and business customers' work life, and can range from major inventions to small innovations in the product's form. Marketing innovations might consist of creative launch events and campaigns.

Innovations demonstrate to customers that the company is a dynamic enterprise that can create new and relevant experiences on an ongoing basis. Innovations can attract new customers; most of the time, however, they build customer equity by helping a company sell more products to existing customers.

Innovations of all kinds need to be planned, managed, and marketed so that they improve the customer experience. In Chapter 7, using cases from my own consulting, I demonstrate how to incorporate experience into new product development and marketing events.

To summarize, the CEM framework consists of five steps. Step 1 (analyzing the experiential world of the customer) is an *analysis* step. Step 2 (building the experiential platform) is a *strategy* step. Steps 3 through 5 (designing the brand experience, structuring the customer interface, and engaging in continuous innovation) are *implementation steps*.

The chapters that follow provide specific ideas and concepts for managing each of the steps as well as methodologies for implementing them. In the remainder of this chapter, I answer key questions that managers have asked me about the framework.

Must Managers Do the Five CEM Steps in Sequence, or Can They Be Done Simultaneously?

In management, you need analysis to formulate strategy, and you need a strategy to guide the implementation. In the CEM framework, analysis precedes strategy, and strategy precedes implementation. There is a natural and logical order here. But what about the three implementation steps? Do they have to be planned and executed in the order presented?

The answer is "not necessarily." In general, they can be managed in parallel, or any step may take priority over any other. In my experience, the order given here is often the easiest and most natural way to implement a CEM project. For example, with an existing brand, changing the brand experience is often easier and quicker to plan and track than restructuring, if not reengineering, the customer interface. In certain projects, however, where transactional encounters heavily determine the experience, structuring the customer interface may take priority over redesigning the brand experience.

Similarly, when launching a new product, and thus starting from scratch with its experience creation, the first thing needed is an appropriate product design. This will determine the look and feel in logos, signage, and packaging as well as the right communications. After this step, we should consider how to sell the product and service it, and how to interrelate with the customer. Then perhaps we should think about the launch event and future innovations. So, in most situations, a step-by-step implementation, starting with the brand experience and followed by the interface and innovation, is appropriate.

What Happens Before and After the CEM Project?

The five steps describe a CEM project comprehensively. The question arises, however, "Is any key input required before the project, and are some actions required afterward?"

The key input and, in fact, often the first question I ask when beginning a CEM project is "What is the objective?" Establishing objectives and keeping track of them as work proceeds are critical factors in the success of any business project, including a CEM project.

Two characteristics usually differentiate good objectives from bad. First, the objectives should be measurable, and the measurement criteria need to be stated (e.g., satisfaction scores or loyalty increases by a certain percentage point; premium pricing above a certain threshold; a certain number of new customers; increased trial by a certain percentage; return on CEM investment). Second, a simple model should be built to show how the quantitative objectives are supposed to be reached through CEM. In Chapter 9, I explain in detail how to build empirical models that guide a CEM project and strategy.

What should happen after a CEM project is completed? Afterward, it is key to fine-tune the experience and to "institutionalize" CEM. The practical CEM framework with its overall philosophy, tools, and methodologies needs to become part of a company's culture through company-wide change-management as well as learning and training initiatives. In Chapter 9, I demonstrate how to include CEM into support systems as well as organizational structures and processes.

What Are the Application Areas of the Framework?

At the beginning of the chapter, we looked briefly at specific business issues the CEM framework can address. Opportunities to apply the CEM framework exist whenever you face a customer-focused issue (e.g., changing customer perceptions because they are out of line with the reality of your offer, increasing customer loyalty and satisfaction, or getting customers to try your new product). But the framework is even more adaptable and useful than that. Often companies encounter problems that initially do not look like customer-experience issues, but on closer examination they may turn out to be just that. In these cases, a CEM project can add tremendous value.

Let's look at five of these situations (see Figure 2.2):

1. *Segmentation and targeting.* For many firms, segmenting customers and selecting targets pose immense challenges. Part of the problem is that the issue is often viewed the wrong way. Many companies do not view segmentation in terms of the customer but from the perspective of the company and its products (by segmenting according to features, price, or distribution channel). Similarly, companies often believe that targeting decisions are sound as long as their analysts have spent enough time and money mining the data for geographic and demographic data structures (in consumer markets) or information on firm size and

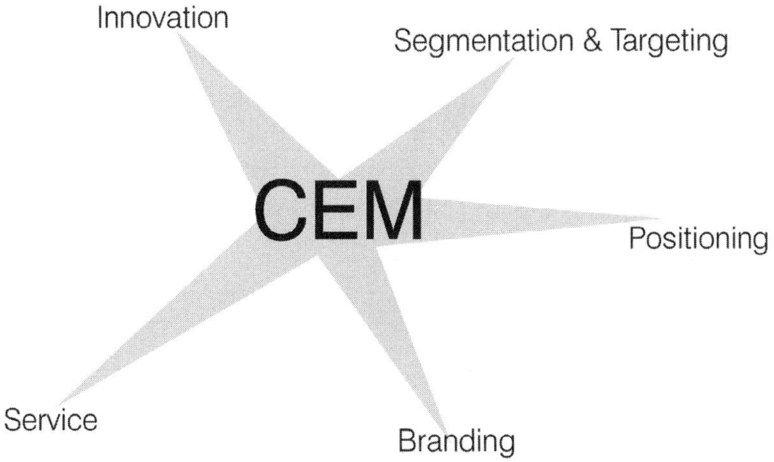

Innovation

Segmentation & Targeting

CEM

Positioning

Service

Branding

FIGURE 2.2
Application Areas of the CEM Framework

profitability (in industrial and B2B markets). Given the immense power of computing and data mining capabilities, this temptation is particularly strong, the notion being "Let's just crank the data, and we'll get the right segmentation and targeting." However, segmentation and targeting decisions without insight into the customer experience are useless and not even executable. As I will show in Chapter 3, the CEM framework approaches segmentation and targeting issues very differently; it starts with research tools that reveal meaningful data by analyzing the experiential worlds offered to consumers as well as business customers.

2. *Positioning.* Another key issue for companies is how to position the corporation, its brands, and its products. Companies often commission perceptual maps (those two-dimensional displays with dots as products and dimensions as lines). But these maps are usually based solely on verbal input and are unrepresentative of customers' daily experiences. Just ask yourself how much insight and guidance for implementation you can derive from the typical two- or three-dimensional perceptual maps with the dimensions labeled "high price—low price," or "high quality—low quality," or "strong image—weak image." Even when the labeling is more specific (e.g., "fresh—processed" for a food product, or "more durable—faster setting" for an industrial adhesive), we still do not know exactly what these terms mean to the customer. We are still unsure of the value they may provide and how they may affect packaging, advertising, the customer interface, and innovations. As

shown in Chapter 4, the CEM framework produces a more meaningful experiential positioning and experiential value proposition, with a theme that can be used to implement packaging, advertising, the interface, and innovations.

3. *Branding.* Many companies have jumped on the branding bandwagon as the magic formula to enhance value. "Let's turn our undifferentiated offer into a strong brand. Let's value the brand and improve the brand image. Let's change the brand's personality." Such initiatives usually lead nowhere. After a couple of years of brand consulting to determine the strengths of the brand; its value; its identity; what it would be like as a person . . . and changing the logo, stationery, and advertising, many brands still fail to connect with the customer and don't sell. Management then realizes that the logo, signage, and advertising were only insignificant parts of the problem. Most branding issues are really *brand experience* issues or, more precisely, issues of the *customer experience with the brand.* To address this predicament effectively requires more than inward soul searching about the meaning of the company and its brands. The company needs, first, to understand the customer's experiential world and, second, to create a differentiated strategy platform that it can implement in an innovative fashion. Chapter 5 shows how CEM accomplishes this by examining a brand in a much more comprehensive fashion than any prior branding framework and implementing the new brand experience in an integrative and creative fashion.

4. *Service.* In most so-called industrialized nations, service-based businesses make up about two-thirds of the economy. Not surprisingly, providing service quality is on everybody's priority list. Most service management, however, is not customer-focused but is based instead on prior untested assumptions about customer preferences for service. Companies may assume that customers will be happiest when they are treated in the most intimate and personalized manner (when in fact they may just seek efficiency) or, conversely, that customers prefer to serve themselves (when they really would appreciate a helping hand). As a result, most service systems are either people- or technology-intensive; rarely do they bring people and technology together to deliver outstanding, memorable, and unique service experiences. As described in Chapter 6, this need not be so. The focus of the CEM approach is on understanding what customer interface is most appropriate for delivering the right service experience.

5. *Innovation.* Although companies face constant pressure to be innovative and to break boundaries, innovation is viewed narrowly, as if it resided only in the R&D department or referred only to technical innovation. Technical innovation in product features is part of the story, but it is not the whole story. Consumers often view innovation in terms of whether a new product, service, or communication helps them improve how they live. Similarly, business customers are focused on whether an innovation improves their way of doing business. As discussed in Chapter 7, customers value innovation, but not just technical innovation oriented toward features and benefits. From the

customer's perspective, small improvements in the customer interface are a major innovation if they simplify or speed up doing business with the company. An appealing line extension that changes the product from powder to liquid can be a breakthrough innovation if it makes the customer's life easier. Even innovations in the look and feel of a product and in experiential communications are important if they make the customer feel better or happier. Why do we so often overlook such innovations? Because we are not focusing on the customer experience! Thus, many issues framed as "innovation challenges" are really challenges to better understand the customer's experiential world, the brand, and the customer interface.

One more point. The five stages of the CEM framework may be seen as structurally equivalent to those of the classic marketing strategy: market analysis, segmentation, targeting, positioning, and implementation in the so-called Four P's (product, price, promotion, and place). However, there are some key differences as well.

First, traditional marketing strategy is product-based, not customer-based. Many traditional marketing managers still believe in product superiority ("the better mousetrap"), where the task is simply to push the product through the channel to the right target. Most marketing departments are organized around product categories and focus on pushing as many units of the same product as possible to any kind of customer. Because repeated selling of desirable products to a specific customer segment is not a primary objective, traditional marketing is not really interested in an in-depth understanding of customers.

Second, the CEM framework is conceptually much tighter and more focused than the classic marketing strategy model, which is a hodgepodge of economic, psychological, and sociological analysis combined with some war metaphors and so-called "strategies." For the most part, it is but a list of factors to consider with few precise concepts and corresponding methodologies. When the model does focus on a specific factor (e.g., on competitive analysis), it gets so bogged down in details (e.g., game theory) that it loses its practical relevance. In contrast, the CEM model strikes the right balance and does not lose track of its goal: the management of the customer experience. If Chapter 1 persuaded you that the customer experience must be the key goal in management and marketing, then CEM provides a rigorous conceptual and methodological approach to achieving that goal.

What Is Unique About the CEM Framework?

An important attribute of the CEM framework is that it focuses on all sorts of customer-related issues. But what makes it unique is *how* the framework focuses on the customer. The CEM framework combines the analytical and the creative, considers both strategy and implementation, and does so externally and internally.

CEM Is Both Analytical and Creative

The CEM framework includes both analytical and creative concepts and tools. Such a combination is highly unusual. The paradigms discussed in Chapter 1 were largely analytical. On the other hand, ad agencies, corporate identity firms, and Web designers provide creative services that are often entirely devoid of analytics. Creative minds and analytical thinkers alike tend to believe that the two worlds are separate and incompatible: creativity cannot be structured or analyzed because it is "intuitive"; and, conversely, analysis, research, and strategy have nothing creative about them.

I disagree. In fact, a business can only develop to its fullest potential when it can merge analysis and creativity. The analytical is necessary for structuring, analyzing, and quantifying issues. Creative considerations are essential for differentiating the business and for catching customers' attention and satisfying their wants and needs.

The CEM framework meshes the worlds of the analytical and the creative. It is rigorous, internally consistent, and well structured. The tools presented in each chapter and the overall model and metrics that link experience to customer equity measures are analytical and possess quantitative components. At the same time, the framework is creative in its use of novel concepts, unique tools, and unusual research techniques for gaining customer insight.

CEM Is Both Strategy and Implementation

Most customer frameworks are concerned either with strategy or with implementation.

Consider the frameworks developed by general management consulting firms (e.g., McKinsey, Boston Consulting Group, Accenture). They operate in the heights of corporate strategy, value chains, and SWOT (strengths, weaknesses, opportunities, threats) analyses or, at best, in the world of broad-based segmentation schemes or generic market positioning maps with dots and vectors. A frequent criticism of consulting firms is that they don't "get their hands dirty." They don't show you, as a manager, what exactly all those analyses and strategies imply for your company. That's up to you to decide after you read the lengthy report, and once you act, you often fail.

Or take the area of branding. The brand-consulting firms create "brand strategy" to build "brand equity." But they usually steer clear of any in-depth customer research. They also avoid providing suggestions for ad communications, packaging, store, or Web design: these tasks belong to the ad agencies, packaging design firms, and interior and Web designers. Nor will branding firms construct a model and metrics to show how the brand repositioning, brand essence, or brand DNA (or whatever the terminology might be) can build customer equity through customer acquisition, retention, and add-on selling.

Unlike most frameworks for managing customers, CEM includes both strategy and implementation in a uniform framework. Strategic considerations are at the core of the first two steps: analyzing the experiential world of the customer and building the experiential platform. Next, three implementation steps focus on the brand experience, the customer interface, and continuous innovation.

Moreover, in the CEM framework, strategy and implementation are tightly linked, as is each step to the next. An analysis of the experiential world of the customer usually results in experiential positioning options for the brand. These are closely examined in Step 2 (Building the experiential platform). The outcome of this study—the experiential platform—serves as a blueprint for the implementation of the core strategy for the brand. It specifies desired outcomes including generalized customer expectations about the product and its look and feel, communications, informational and service requirements, and ways to enhance the experience through additional offers that fit the usage situation. All of these considerations are tremendously helpful for implementing the brand experience and the customer interface as well as for creating continuous innovation.

CEM's Focus Is External and Internal

The foremost concern of CEM is the external (customer) experience. In the CEM framework, we analyze both end consumers and B2B customers and design strategy and implementations for them. However, CEM is also concerned with the "internal customer" (the employee experience). There is a simple reason for this concern: How employees feel and experience the company and its initiatives is critical for delivering the right brand experiences (e.g., through communications), enhancing the customer interface (face-to-face and via the call-center), and encouraging continuous innovation initiatives.

This commitment to the employee experience is not a generic, empty human resources statement about empowerment. The internal focus calls for specific practices, rewards, and incentives, as well as measurement and promotional systems.

Conclusion

The CEM framework goes far beyond prior marketing and management approaches that call themselves customer-oriented and is unique in how it focuses on customers.

With the CEM framework and its methodologies, you can integrate the experience across various touchpoints to link tangible outcome measures and manage both the external customer and internal (employee) customer experience. The framework addresses internal and external business issues including segmentation and targeting, positioning, branding, service, and innovation.

In Chapters 3 through 7, you get specific details for using each step of the CEM framework to manage the customer experience. Then, in Chapter 8, you learn about the power of seamless integration—how you can merge the different aspects of the customer experience so that your customers feel fully connected at every touchpoint. Finally, Chapter 9 provides models and metrics to link the customer experience to "customer equity" (i.e., the financial value of the customer for your company over the course of the customer's lifetime). When you enhance customer equity through CEM, you engage in premium pricing; you enjoy the benefits of customer loyalty; and you have lower acquisition costs and increased retention. As a result, revenues, profits, and the financial value of the firm increase. This final chapter also presents some of the internal, organizational requirements for successful CEM and how they relate to the external experience.

Analyzing the Experiential World of the Customer

Many companies have an internal focus instead of a customer-oriented view. They devote enormous resources to developing new products and technologies with little customer input. Their communications extol product features but often lack a message that connects with customers. Their service centers are not set up to act efficiently on customer input and feedback. In fact, at times they seem to be afraid of it. After all, customer input and feedback might challenge some of the company's preconceived notions about the superiority of its product or service.

FIGURE 3.1
Interior of Carnegie Hall's Isaac Stern Auditorium. *Credit:* Don Perdue.

FIGURE 3.2
Exterior of Carnegie Hall.
Credit: Don Perdue.

FIGURE 3.3

View from stage of Carnegie Hall's Isaac Stern Auditorium. *Credit:* Don Perdue.

FIGURE 3.4

View from stage, end stage configuration: Judy and Arthur Zankel Hall. Computer Visuals by dbox for Polshek Partnership Architects.

This situation needs to change. Companies need to become more responsive to customers and incorporate customer insight into their strategies and implementations. They need to use customer input when they design the brand experience, customer interface, and when they launch new products. They need to use customer feedback to improve experiences. To do this, companies need to learn how to see the world from the customer's point of view.

In this chapter, you'll find concepts and methodologies for analyzing the experiential world of the customer. These concepts and methodologies provide critical customer insight for segmentation and targeting, and for the communication and implementation phases of CEM. Moreover, case examples show how successful companies discard their own preconceptions and focus on understanding what happens in the broader contexts of consumers' lives or a business customer's enterprise.

A CEM project that I conducted for Carnegie Hall and a project for British Petroleum illustrate what it means to focus on the customer's experiential world and how research can give you insight into that world.

Carnegie Hall: Understanding the Concert-Going Experience

For every musician, New York's Carnegie Hall is not just another location, place, or concert hall. It is, in the words of the late violinist Isaac Stern, a "unique experience." But what experiences do the concert goers have when they attend a concert at Carnegie Hall?

In 2002, I conducted an experiential project for Carnegie Hall to understand the experience of one of the world's major concert venues. The project was part of a broader effort that Carnegie Hall was making to understand its brand better. The organization had conducted opinion and attitude research in the past and, in parallel to the research described here, was again conducting an opinion survey on its brand. This standard research, however, produced only a partial picture of the Carnegie Hall brand. Management needed a better understanding of the actual concert-going experience: what customers notice and experience at a concert; how they feel when they enter and leave the hall; what they do during the intermission; and how the Carnegie Hall brand comes to life at these different touchpoints.

The project consisted of three parts that tracked the customer's experience before, during, and after a musical performance. Before the performance, participants (current subscribers and other music lovers) met in a focus group. They then attended a performance together with the researcher team. During the performance, they shared with the researchers their observations and experiences of the hall and of Carnegie Hall promotional materials. Immediately after the performance, participants reassembled and discussed their experiences; they also engaged in a creative task—the construction of a visual board that represented their Carnegie Hall experience.

When participants first arrived at Carnegie Hall, they completed a short background questionnaire about their past experiences with the organization. The moderator of the focus group prompted participants to think not only about the quality of the performances that they had attended but also about experiences that occurred outside the hall and the performance itself: How easy was it to purchase tickets? Did they visit the Web site, and did they like it? Did they enjoy the gift shop, the cocktail bar, and the ambience of the whole place? Moreover, participants were asked to compare their experiences at Carnegie Hall with those at other performance spaces such as Avery Fisher Hall, part of Lincoln Center in New York. The researchers captured these conversations with research participants on video.

During the concert experience, researchers accompanied pairs of participants and recorded their impressions with a digital audio device. As participants entered the hall and looked for their seats, the researchers asked about the experience of arriving at and entering the hall. During the breaks between the concert pieces, the researchers asked about the overall atmosphere of the hall, the acoustics, and the audience. At intermission, the groups dispersed to different areas of the hall to gain participants' insights about the gift shop, the bar areas, even restrooms. Again, participants were asked to share their thoughts and experiences. They also discussed the printed program and the brochures for the coming season.

While walking back to the focus group facility after the concert, participants commented on the quality of the performance that they had attended and made suggestions for improvements. They then worked together to construct a visual board selecting images that represented their concert going experience at Carnegie Hall. At the end, they were shown a sketch of Judy and Arthur Zankel Hall, a new performance space to be opened in Carnegie Hall in 2003 (see Figure 3.4).

Our research into the experiential world of the customer revealed several key insights that would have been difficult, if not impossible, to obtain through traditional methods. Overall, patrons felt very positive about the core experience of the concert—the auditorium, the acoustics, and the performances. They thought, however, that the surrounding elements—such as the amenities during intermission—needed improvement. Some of the insights reflected small details that could enhance the concert-going experience. Patrons suggested installing telephones in the lobby, managing the queues at the bar areas better, improving the speed of the elevator service, and providing better lighting at the seats to make it easier to read the program. Although these details may seem minor, such insights offer a glimpse into the experiential world of the customer and can actually make or break the experience for some.

The research also revealed significant room for improvement in the printed program. Older people complained that the small font made it hard to read. Some found that the ads overwhelmed the information about the music and the performers. Others thought that the cover was a hodgepodge of fonts. Overall, many research participants found the program adequate, but "nothing special." This insight is worth considering: perhaps Carnegie Hall should develop a printed program as special as the rest of the concert experience.

Of broader interest were insights into the Carnegie Hall experience from first-time visitors. They enjoyed the intimacy of the hall and reported that a feeling of closeness to the performers set Carnegie Hall apart from other performance venues. They also praised the décor for being elegant and understated, "not too flashy"—an important and perhaps counterintuitive finding in this age of excess and over stimulation. Concertgoers provided some useful insights about the new performance space in Zankel Hall. Many felt it provided an opportunity for Carnegie Hall to deliver new types of programming while maintaining the strength of the Carnegie Hall brand. Several patrons recommended using the new hall to promote diverse forms of music. Many also felt Zankel Hall could attract younger audiences as well as give opportunities to young, upcoming artists.

This experiential research provided Carnegie Hall with information about its patrons and the concert going experience that laid the groundwork for both minor adjustments and major initiatives. Only CEM can provide this level of insight into the customer experience.

BP Connect: Improving the Experience at the Pump

As part of a global repositioning and rebranding of the BP brand (from "British Petroleum" to "Beyond Petroleum"), the company was looking for a new service station model that would demonstrate its commitment to innovation and progressiveness. In the U.S. market, the challenge was twofold: BP had acquired Amoco and needed both a special offer that would retain loyal Amoco customers and a cutting-edge brand communication strategy to build awareness, appeal, and credibility.

The target customer for the service station, the design of the station, and the related communication program were based on research conducted by Penn, Schoen, and Berland, a market research firm. For this project, Penn, Schoen, and Berland

FIGURE 3.5
BP Connect service station. *Credit:* Goes Photo 2002.

used a range of innovative research techniques to gain insight into the daily lifestyles of the prime target segment.

In the early stages of the project, focus group and quantitative retail exploration studies were conducted with members of different target segments in the United States and the United Kingdom to identify shopping and errand patterns in people's daily routines. Researchers asked participants where they went to satisfy their needs when they ran out of things or wanted a quick lunch or dinner. They also asked specifically about participants' use of convenience stores. The study revealed that more and more categories of retailers were developing channels to capitalize on the convenience market. Supermarkets offered sandwiches and prepared foods and express checkout lanes;

FIGURE 3.6
BP Connect convenience store. *Credit:* Goes Photo 2002.

drugstores provided cookies and snacks, and even sandwiches in the United Kingdom; finally, some grocery stores and discount retailers like Wal-Mart were selling gasoline. At the same time, the research revealed an apparent opportunity to create an experience theme around a high-quality one-stop offer for quality-conscious customers who were pressed for time. Such an offer would enable BP to compete and differentiate not only against other service stations, but also against other kinds of retail outlets.

Next, qualitative and quantitative store studies were conducted among motorists to test specific designs, features, and offers and to explore potential communications and messages. In one part of the research, participants responded to store designs (exterior and interior) as well as to various in-store offerings (gourmet coffee, fresh sandwiches, and an e-kiosk). In the next part, they visited a prototype store, pumped gas, used the e-kiosk, and got coffee. Overall, respondents were enthusiastic, becoming involved and suggesting changes in the features of the store. This research phase was invaluable for fine-tuning the experience.

BP also conducted advertising-related studies to test the ad concept, production versions of the ads, media strategy, and the effectiveness of the campaign. Mall test interviews with 527 respondents in the United States and the United Kingdom provided key insights for selecting an experiential communication theme that included women and situations they could relate to. For the media strategy, a quantitative study involving 1,500 interviews tracked the activities, energy level, and moods over the day of the "Spiderwoman" target (women whose jobs and family responsibilities left them in need of convenience solutions). The results of this research helped BP save costs and advertise more effectively by avoiding expensive big-name TV shows. Instead, BP designed an integrated campaign using radio, TV, outdoor, and on-site advertising, each responding to the target consumer's moods and needs at a particular moment. The effectiveness of this campaign was tracked with a "deep dive" trade area study that interviewed only target customers who lived within 2.5 miles of a new BP Connect station.

The "BP Connect" project was a winner by every measure: awareness, usage, and sales were up; new consumers instantly bonded to the brand and Amoco loyalists did not defect; and the company gained market share not only from other oil companies but also from retail venues such as supermarkets and drugstores. The research firm won the 2002 David Ogilvy Award of the Advertising Research Foundation for its work on BP Connect. By probing the experiential world of the customer, Penn, Schoen, and Berland set the stage for BP's brilliantly successful experiential initiative.

Companies Need Customer Insight

As the Carnegie Hall and BP Connect cases demonstrate, analyzing the experiential world of the customer is the starting point for obtaining vital customer insight. Companies need such insight to develop an experiential platform and successful implementation. Customer insight enables a company to position a product with the right features, appeal, communications, and customer interface.

Companies in many industries are keen on developing customer insight:

- The pharmaceutical industry and medical community need customer insight when marketing lifestyle drugs and treatments such as Viagra (targets impotence), Xenical (controls weight), and Botox (diminishes the appearance of facial lines and wrinkles). Marketing these products requires that companies consider not only the immediate effects of the drug (its functional features and benefits) but also the patient's values, self-concept, workstyle, and lifestyle. For example, how important is sexuality as part of the patient's life? How sexually active would the patient like to be? What is the patient's body self-image and ideal weight, and how much can it fluctuate over time? How does the patient feel about the effects of aging, and how does he or she define beauty and attractiveness? These are the kinds of questions I ask immediately whenever a company approaches me about an experiential project for such treatments. In this light, "patients" become "consumers" who discuss their consumption needs in consultation with a medical professional, instead of being the "objects" of the doctor and the pharmaceutical industry.

- Technology companies need new insights and a deeper understanding of their customers, young ones in particular. The era when the same radio sat on the cabinet in the living room for 20 years is long gone. Today's young consumers of Gen X and Gen Y—and even the aging baby boomers—are using radios, CD and MP3 players, DVD players, and digital cameras when they hike, skydive, skateboard, or skate in the park (and afterward, when they wait for attention in the emergency room). Technology products are fast becoming experiential lifestyle products, and they should be researched and marketed accordingly.

- The consumer durables industry (e.g., washers, dryers, refrigerators) faces the reverse issue: how to incorporate technology that enhances the customer experience into the washing, drying, and cooling products that are so much a part of people's daily lives. Since the late 1990s, "information appliances" have been the focus of intense development efforts. Several companies have been experimenting with Internet-connected appliances to fully integrate the Web into people's daily lives. An example is a Web-connected refrigerator developed by Sun Microsystems, featuring a "desktop" with virtual

Post-it notes and a handy calculator. On the verge of the new millennium, some analysts predicted that sales of non-PC Internet devices would reach 11 million units by 2004. Will sales like this really materialize? Maybe, if the experience is right . . . if these companies do the necessary homework to understand how today's husbands and wives, and the rest of the population, go about their household chores.

These examples illustrate that analyzing and understanding the experiential world of the customer is key for developing products and marketing them appropriately, and not only in a business-to-consumer (B2C) context. B2B marketers and managers can also profit from such an understanding, as described later in this chapter.

But how exactly can you go about analyzing the experiential world of the customer? I suggest using the following steps:

1. Identify the precise target customer for the planned experience. Unless you can pinpoint your customers, your efforts to tailor effective experiences for them will miss the mark.
2. Divide the experiential world. Using the customer's perspective, tease out what I call the "four layers of the customer's experiential world."
3. Track the entire experience along all the touchpoints between the customer and the company, from awareness of the product right through its purchase, usage, and disposal.
4. Survey the competitive landscape and examine how competition can affect the customer experience.

Identify the Target Customer

A precise identification of your target customer is the first step in analyzing the experiential world. Different customer targets (business customers vs. end consumers) require different experiences. The kind of experience customers want also will reflect whether the purchaser will actually be the user of the product, how often the customer uses a product, and how loyal he or she is to a given brand.

Consumers versus Business Customers

Broadly speaking, for any business there are two types of customers: individual consumers, who use a product as part of their daily lives, and business customers including distributors, wholesalers, and retailers. The latter group also includes customers who can influence the success of a business even though they may not be sales targets themselves—investors, media and the press, government agencies, and so on. This kind of analysis is Business 101.

What is important here is that these two types of customers are not just different targets in the channel of distribution. From an experiential perspective, end consumers and business customers are radically different entities because they expect very different experiences. Why? Partly because their goals are not the same: individual consumers are often acting to meet personal needs; business customers are acting on behalf of a firm to meet a business goal. As part of your analysis, you must take these differences into account.

Typically, the end consumer is affected—consciously or unconsciously—by product design, branding, advertising campaigns, personal forms of relationship management, and in-novation initiatives of the manufacturer or service provider in a lifestyle context. The end consumer goes to the stores, compares products, tries one or another, may make an impulse purchase, or may just window-shop for fun. End consumers make rational decisions about a purchase at times, but they are just as likely to be motivated by emotion, intuition, and impulse.

Business customers behave quite differently. For the business customer, buying is a job. Also, the business buyer is unlikely to use the product. As a retailer, the business customer may su-pervise the unloading of the product and stocking it on the shelves. As service staff, the customer may have to sell or repair the product. Usually, what counts for business customers is whether they can use the product to produce other value added (other products that are sold on to the next channel member) and whether they can run a successful business doing so. This sums up their experience with the product, and as a result, they will judge a firm based on whether it provides that experience.

Most businesses have to service both types of customers. A manufacturer of a product, for example, will deal with both the trade and the end consumer, and therefore needs to under-stand both worlds. If the manufacturer fails to understand the retailer's world and cannot motivate the retailer to sell the product, sales will suffer. On the other hand, if the product doesn't appeal to consumers in the first place because it fails to deliver the right experience for them, no amount of retailer motivation and "push" will do the trick.

What is more, the two customer worlds are often inter-twined and interdependent. If a product experience fails to please end consumers, a retailer may be flooded with service complaints. In this situation, the business customer experience will suffer, and the retailer may stop carrying the product. No one has had a good experience, and everyone is unhappy. This may happen, for example, with a new PDA (personal digital assistant), that turns out to be unreliable and difficult to use. End consumers will be unhappy and return the product to retailers. Retailers will be buried in returned items, and unless the manufacturer can cover the loss, they may think twice about ordering the next new product from that manufacturer. Everyone loses. To succeed, then, businesses have to be sensitive to both end consumers and business customers.

Purchasers and Users

Often, there may be more than one business-customer or end-consumer target. A chain of customers may be involved in the decision making, purchase, and consumption of products. Marketers have assigned roles to members of such chains: "influencers," "decision makers," "information collectors," and, of course, "buyers" and "users." Naturally, the last two tend to get the most attention, but the others can be equally important.

Shifting from one target role to another, or focusing on a previously ignored target role, can provide new growth for a company. Bloomberg, which has become one of the largest and most profitable business-information providers, has done exactly that. Before Bloomberg, Reuters dominated the industry. It provided news and real-time prices to the brokerage community and focused on the buyers of the system, the information technology managers who valued standardization. Bloomberg focused instead on the users, the traders and analysts, and provided a better experience for them: easy-to-use terminals, keyboards labeled with financial terms, flat-panel monitors, built-in analytic capabilities—the interface that all hobby traders now can have at their fingertips but that hardly existed before Bloomberg. In the 1980s, the dark ages of trading, traders literally had to download information and use a pencil and calculator to do financial calculations. In addition to providing financial information at the stroke of a key, Bloomberg has enhanced the experience of traders who work long hours with added services that help them in their personal lives (travel arrangements, real estate searches, florists, etc.). By recognizing that the experience of users matters, Bloomberg has built an empire where before there was nothing.

Usage and Loyalty Groups

There are still other ways of looking at customers. Two considerations, rate of usage and customer loyalty, are especially useful because they determine the richness, intensity, and variety of an experience.

Charting rate of usage is critical. Experiences are likely to be different—and to be driven by different factors—depending on whether the customer is using a product for the first time or is a repeat user. For example, the first time you ride a motorcycle, a sense of safety may be key; if you have been riding for five years, you may be more interested in speed and performance. In a very different product category, the first time you see the opera *Aida*, you are likely to be impressed by all the razzle-dazzle in the Triumph scene (the huge chorus, the horses, Radames riding in on a chariot). However, after you have seen your twentieth *Aida*, the Triumph scene alone may not do it for you: you will look for the subtler aspects of the production such as how the forbidden relationship between Radames and Aida is portrayed. The first time you get a loan from the bank, you may put up with any form of customer "dis-service"; it feels great just to get the loan. The fourth or fifth time, you may evaluate your experience based on speed and convenience.

Loyalty is another variable. If you have always consumed a particular product from the same company, your experience is likely to be different than if you try different brands all the time or switch back and forth. Through comparison shopping, switchers gain knowledge about product differences and often become attuned to features and price. To capture their attention requires focusing on the right experience relative to the ones that competitors provide, especially for product features and price. In contrast, the loyal customer is likely to know the experience in detail and is satisfied with it. With this customer, it becomes important not to change the product too much or too fast.

Because experiences depend on frequency of usage and loyalty, a company either must do its experiential analysis broadly, designing an experience that includes all sorts of customer bases, or be specific about the sample of analysis (based on the strategic objectives for certain target customers).

Rate of usage and loyalty are key customer characteristics in the travel destination business. Imagine you work for the tourist board of a major city or resort area. Very likely, first-time visitors expect a different experience (in terms of attractions, lodging, and entertainment) than do the loyalists who visit every year. In addition, there are likely to be differences between the experienced traveler and the customer who seldom travels.

Divide the Experiential World into Four Layers

In *Experiential Marketing,* I argued that we often focus too narrowly on the product and extol its features and benefits in advertising and communications. I suggested that we can broaden our thinking by using the concept that I call the "sociocultural consumption vector" (SCCV). Thinking of a product in terms of the SCCV, instead of just features, provides a more complete description and understanding because the SCCV includes the consumption situation of the product and important trends in the sociocultural environment. The SCCV contextualizes the product by encompassing other key elements of the experiential world of the customer.

How exactly can we do this? Analytically, we can divide the customer's world into four layers, starting with a broad-based, general outer layer and continuing through more specific layers until we reach the brand experience.

The Four Layers of the Experiential World

In my teaching and consulting work, I have found it useful to distinguish the following four layers (see Figure 3.7):

1. The broad-based experience associated with the customer's sociocultural context (in consumer markets) or the business context (in business-to-business markets).
2. The experience provided by the usage or consumption situation of the brand.
3. The experience provided by the product category.
4. The experience provided by the brand.

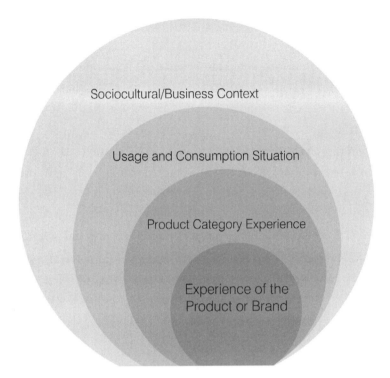

FIGURE 3.7
The Four Layers of the Experiential World

Let's look at an example, a brand of razors or razor blades, starting with the specific experience provided by the brand and then moving up toward the broader levels. The brand experience is how the razor looks and feels in your hands when you are shaving. This brand experience, in part, is driven by the product category, although this particular brand may have unique features (e.g., three blades instead of two, for a technologically enhanced shave). More importantly, the brand and the product category are embedded in the broader consumption situation of shaving and grooming in the morning.

Finally, this consumption situation (shaving and grooming) is part of a sociocultural context that includes activities that a man or woman undertakes to get ready for work and to "appear professional" or "lead a professional life." By moving from the specific to the broader layers, we are increasing our understanding of what a razor and razor blade mean to today's customers. Once incorporated into the context of a person's professional life, products as small and seemingly insignificant as a razor and razor blades assume new meaning and provide us with new marketing opportunities.

Now consider a B2B example, an inventory-planning software program. The brand experience of the software may include how well it works; how easy it is to use, upgrade, and get technical support; and how easily it can be coordinated with other software packages. The broader usage context is the firm's enterprise-resource planning software and the experience of running an enterprise-wide system. The broad-based business contexts are the objectives and strategies of the firm. So to arrive at a genuine understanding of the user experience for this inventory software package, we need to understand how well it fits into the firm's overall objectives and strategy.

Customers receive stimuli that trigger experiences at all four layers, and these stimuli are often associated with different delivery media. In consumer markets, media that trigger experiences at the sociocultural level include books, movies, events, and magazines. At the usage level of the category are lifestyle magazines. Media that serve as triggers at the product and brand level include specific consumer magazines (e.g., fashion, sports, music, or home magazines) or brand media (product information, packaging, brand ads, etc.).

In B2B markets, media that trigger experiences at the business-environment level include business reports on TV, annual reports, and noticeable technology trends featured in such media. At the usage level, general business magazines are important. At the product and brand level, trade media may feature product catalogs and reports.

When using the four-layer approach to divide the experiential world, the brand—which is the center of our attention—is related to the three other layers of the experiential world. The brand experience is developed out of an understanding of the broadest layer of sociocultural trends. The brand fits perfectly into the usage situation. Moreover, the brand offers a differentiated experience within the product category.

As a result, the customer will perceive the brand to be meaningful and relevant. End consumers will see the brand as enriching their daily lives; business customers will feel that the brand helps them solve their business problems.

A Methodology for Layering the Experiential World

In my consulting practice, I have developed a methodology for layering the experiential world of the customer. The core objective of this methodology is to generate a clear picture of the four layers of the experiential world and then to funnel the broader layers into more specific ones.

We start constructing the four layers of the experiential world with the outer ring, by examining pertinent lifestyles (in a B2C context) or business trends (in a B2B context). The analysis and research at this stage (using research techniques described at the end of this chapter) address three key questions related to the nature of each identified trend, the people behind each trend (the trendsetters), and how each trend relates to a certain usage situation. It is useful to include diverse experts in the research. For each of the three key issues, it is necessary to answer a set of questions:

- *Nature of the trend.* How can we describe this trend precisely? What are the indications that the trend will continue? How significant is the trend? Has it happened before? What is different now? Are there any overlaps with other identified trends?
- *The trendsetters.* Who launched the trend? Who are the future drivers of the trend? Who will diffuse the trend?
- *The trend in usage.* How does/could the trend manifest itself in a certain product usage situation? What is reflective of this trend in a particular usage situation?

Answering these questions is critical for funneling the outer ring (the trend) into the adjacent inner ring (the usage situation). For the usage situation, we research and answer the following questions:

- *Nature of the usage situation.* How important is this usage situation? What elements of the usage situation reflect the trend? How could the brand enrich the usage situation?
- *The users.* Which type of user engages in this usage situation? What does the user do to be part of this usage situation? What other aspects of the user's personal or professional life affect this usage situation?

- *The usage applied to the brand.* What role does the brand play in this usage situation? How well does the brand fit into this usage situation? How would it fit better?

Finally, we need to funnel the usage situation, which is now experientially enriched by the trend, into the specific inner rings of the product-category and brand experience. To do this, we research the following questions about the product and brand:

- *Nature of the product category and brand.* What is the essence of the product and brand? What are the brand personality and core associations? How can they be merged with the new trend for a particular usage situation?
- *Users of the product category and brand.* Who are the category and brand loyalists and enthusiasts? How could they bring the identified trend to the brand? Which new customers could be helpful in diffusing the trend?

Throughout this funneling process, we need to remain open and think broadly. New ideas, especially if they stretch the current brand positioning, should not be rejected out of hand but used for inspiration.

This layering methodology usually results in several options that you can research further using original experiential qualitative and quantitative techniques. Most important, after you have constructed a layered description of the experiential world, you can track the experience—and enrich it—at the customer touchpoints that exist between the company and the customer. Here is how it is done.

Track the Experience along Touchpoints

The key objective of tracking the experience at customer touchpoints is to develop an understanding of how an experience can be enriched for the customer throughout what marketers call the "customer decision-making process." It starts with the need recognition for the product; continues with information search, information processing, and choice; and culminates in the purchase. After the purchase, the customer uses the product and ultimately disposes of it before buying a new one, either the same brand or a product in the same or a new category. Each stage of the decision process provides a touchpoint with the customer, and at each touchpoint it is worthwhile finding out not only what information needs customers have (as most traditional marketing has done) but also what experiences they desire.

How can we do this? Ian MacMillan and my colleague at Columbia Business School, Rita McGrath, suggest asking the classic series of simple questions—"what?" "where?" "who?" "when?" and "how?"—at various stages of the decision process.[1] These authors have illustrated their approach using the candle market:

- What are customers doing at each point of the decision process? When do they perceive a need: do they perceive a need only on certain occasions (birthdays) but not others (dinner, warm buffet dishes, power outages) and as a result only search for certain candles, and buy and use certain ones? How could this need perception be changed by suggesting new experiences and applications in a store?

- Where are customers when they are in different stages of the decision situation? Are they at home when the need arises? In the store? Online? How can we make the candle-buying experience most fun and pleasurable?

- Who makes the decision at each decision point, and what experiences do they prefer when they process the information, make a choice, buy, use, and dispose of the product?

- When (time of the day, week, and year) are customers making decisions? Do they feel differently about candles during the day than at night or in the summer and winter? Will it help us as a candle company when we reach them during the best time?

- How are customers' experiences currently addressed at each stage of the decision process?

By differentiating the experience at every stage of the decision process, Blyth Industries, a candle manufacturer, has grown from $2 million U.S. sales to over $500 million globally. As MacMillan and McGrath put it, "not bad for an industry that was in decline for 400 years."

Survey the Competitive Landscape

Competition in experiences is becoming widespread. Talk to hoteliers about their guestrooms. Talk to airline executives about their lounges. Talk to car manufacturers about the interiors of their cars and showrooms. Everyone is eager to find out what new customer experiences their competitors are coming up

---

Box 3.1

AVIS: MANAGING THE CUSTOMER EXPERIENCE FROM PICK-UP TO DROP-OFF

Renting a car isn't always the most pleasant experience. But Avis is changing all that. In a campaign designed to improve the customer experience at every touchpoint, Avis has transformed the car rental experience and has won record customer loyalty in the process.

How did Avis do it? Put simply, the company undertook to make the entire rental experience, piece by piece, satisfying for its customers. With the help of outside consultants, Avis first isolated a set of factors that car renters care most about. Then they broke down the rental process into 100 discrete steps and proceeded to improve each one of them. Customers care about speed, so Avis initiated the Avis Preferred service program, which allows members to skip the airport check-in counter altogether and go right to the lot. To help customers deal with travel-induced stress, Avis created special "communication centers" in airports around the country, areas where customers can make phone calls, plug in their laptops, make photocopies, and just generally get caught up. To keep customers informed, Avis displays flight information in many of its offices. Computerized kiosks allow customers to get driving directions to wherever they are going.

Avis hasn't neglected the role its employees play in the customer experience, either. Counter personnel are trained to be sensitive to the special needs and interests of individual renters. Rental agents inform parents with small children about the availability of car seats; they provide weather

---

70

Box 3.1   Continued

reports and maps to local golf courses to renters carrying a set of clubs. Avis misses no opportunity to improve the individual customer experience, whatever that may be. What's more, to reassure customers that everything is running smoothly, Avis managers wear headsets. In the words of Diane Karl, vice president for quality assurance and customer care, "Stress levels go down when customers see there's someone in charge. Those headsets are a signal."

What is the outcome of all this attention to the customer experience? In 2002, Avis was ranked number one in its category by the Brand Keys customer loyalty index, an annual survey of brand loyalty for 158 companies in almost 30 different industries. Number one? Not too shabby for a company that built its reputation on being number two. Imagine what customer experience management could do for your company.

Thomas Mucha, "The Payoff for Trying Harder," *Business 2.0* (July 2002), pp. 84–86.

---

with and how to respond to them. Competitive games are no longer played just over price but also over experiences. Therefore, survey the competitive landscape regularly and use what you learn to shape your next move.

You cannot conduct analysis of the experiential world in a competitive void. Customers perceive commercial offers in reference to what key competitors do and what experiences they provide. You need to understand the experiences your competitors are offering your customers. You need to engage in experiential benchmarking. Specifically, you need to survey the experiences offered by three generic types of competitors:

1. *Direct competitors.* What customer experiences do your direct competitors (companies in the same industry and category) provide? Are they better, the same, or worse than the ones you offer? How can you describe the experiences qualitatively? How are customers being treated? What can you learn from your competitors' experiential initiatives?

2. *New entrants.* New entrants into the market need to differentiate themselves. Are they competing on price, functionality, or experiences? What appeals do they use to attract customers? What can you learn from them?

3. *Players outside your industry.* In many ways, this is where most of the inspiration comes from. Competitive benchmarking outside the industry can be most rewarding. Ask yourself, despite all the differences between them and us, how could we use the best from their experience to improve the experiences of our customers?

Westin's Heavenly Bed, Bath, and Crib: Making the Ordinary Extraordinary

Imagine for a moment that you are a hotel manager in the luxury business travelers industry. This is just one industry where competition is no longer about the standard functional attributes of price and location but about the experience—the size of fitness clubs; how guests are welcomed and greeted; the staffing and facilities of business centers; quantity, quality, and type of restaurant facilities; and the size, style, and amenities of the room, bed, and bath. Now imagine a competitor comes out with an experiential campaign about "the bed" and "the bath" in its hotels and implements the experience worldwide. This will redefine how business travelers think from now on about the bed and the bath.

In the late 1990s, Starwood Hotels & Resorts Worldwide, Inc., under its Westin brand decided to give guests the best possible sleeping experience, and launched The Heavenly Bed®. Starwood selected the name "heavenly bed" because the linens of the bed were white to exude serenity and cleanliness. This bedding thus stood out from the brown, patterned bedspreads in most hotels.

The bed's design was based on research and an understanding of the customer experience, and in particular that of the business executive. In a phone survey of 600 executives, respondents said that a good night's sleep was the most important service a hotel could provide. In fact, a large majority said that they missed their own bed more than they missed their spouse.

"Saying something has 900 coils or 250 thread count sheets doesn't jump off the page," said K. C. Kavanagh, vice president of public relations for Starwood Hotels & Resorts. The best method of persuasion was to get customers to experience the beds. Nationwide, the bed began to appear at strange, attention-getting places, as part of a clever experiential PR campaign designed by Jack Morton, an experience communication firm. On Wall Street, brokers were greeted by 30 downy beds lined up in front of the New York Stock Exchange. Commuters could test 20 beds in New York's Grand Central Station. In Savannah, Georgia, skydivers landed on a bed on a barge secured in front of the Westin Savannah Harbour Resort. At the Westin Resort & Spa, located at the Whistler ski resort in British Columbia, the bed careened down a ski mountain suitably named Seventh Heaven. The bed climbed its way into the observatory of Seattle's Space Needle. Through a witty and provocative mass media campaign, with the catchy tagline "Who's the best in bed?" Westin achieved 67 million radio and TV impressions and 124 million print and Web impressions.

Cleanliness perceptions rose from 8.28 to 8.60 and guest room décor from 7.25 to 8.36 on a 10-point satisfaction scale. Just changing the bed also resulted in a higher level of overall hotel satisfaction, which rose by 12 percent after the bed was installed. Guests commented, "It was like my bed at home," or "I won't stay in a hotel that doesn't have a Heavenly Bed," and many wanted to purchase one. Such expectations forced the company to install the beds internationally, and Starwood found it virtually impossible to obtain enough beds to refurnish all its hotels at once.

The campaign was such a success that Westin rolled out "line extension" experiences: the Heavenly Bath[SM] and the Heavenly Crib[SM].

The Heavenly Bath is designed to provide travelers with a therapeutic shower spa and luxurious bath amenities. Westin invested $10 million in new showerheads, curved shower curtain rods, shower curtains, spa towels, luxurious velour bathrobes, and custom amenities in 23,000 of its rooms at 72 Northern American hotels. The company spent a year researching the concept and tested more than 150 showerheads.

According to Barry S. Sternlicht, Chairman and CEO of Starwood Hotels & Resorts Worldwide, Inc., "The hotel

FIGURE 3.8
Westin's Heavenly Bed. *Credit:* Westin Hotels & Resorts © 1999.

industry has typically cut corners in bathrooms, which is ridiculous because next to a great night's sleep, a terrific shower is the most important service a hotel can provide. As a frequent traveler, nothing frustrates me more than waking up in a hotel to a shower with terrible water pressure, a thimble of cheap shampoo, and a scratchy bath towel that looks more like a washcloth. The Heavenly Bath is designed to be the best bath experience in the hotel business, and a better shower than most people have in their homes—a bit of heaven on the road."

The Heavenly Crib is also supposed to improve the experience of the youngest customers—the children—and the experience of the real customer, the parent, along with it. The Heavenly Crib features 100 percent cotton-fitted sheets and a sturdy mattress with coils that offers a superior sleep experience to traditional foam mattresses commonly used in hotel cribs. To enhance the experience for the parents and their kids, Westin staff was specially trained in the set-up, maintenance, and repair of the sleep system and in explaining the use of the crib to the parents.

Competitive experiential initiatives such as Westin's Heavenly Bed, Bath, and Crib put constraints on your own experiential initiatives. Thus, competitors' moves certainly need to be part of your analysis. An experience perspective offers several options for the research that you might commission and the strategy that you might develop. For example, you could start a nasty experiential comparative campaign: "Our beds are just as good! Just look at the stats." (But remember, as we've heard, it's not all about the stats.) Or you could try to copy them; be careful, though, you may end up in court (see

Chapter 5). You could try to focus on another part of the room (but note there is not much left: They already have the bed and bath and even the crib). Unless you want to cheapen your brand and settle for "price differentiation," the only choice is to create an alternative: a different and even more desirable experience. You need to incorporate the experiences provided by customers into your own thinking and bring General Electric's "Kill your own business" mentality to experiences.

Research Techniques for Understanding the Experiential World

We have now examined a four-step process for analyzing the experiential world of the customer. As part of the analysis, it is necessary to conduct primary research with customers.

Using appropriate research techniques and collecting the right data for understanding the experiential world of the customer is not an easy job. Understandably, some managers have taken the easy way out: They say they don't need customer research. They believe that customers can't give the company useful information and original ideas.

The problem is not the customer, but traditional customer research. Most customer research techniques are rigorous by traditional marketing research standards (e.g., reliability and validity). But they lack realism, originality, and the depth of information that we require for relevant insight into the customer experience.

We therefore cannot apply focus groups, one-on-one interviews, or telephone surveys without adapting them; we need to adjust such procedures to gain valuable information about the customer experience.

Three adjustments, in particular, are critical for conducting relevant research on the experiential world of the customer:

1. *Conduct research in natural environments.* Most traditional marketing research is conducted in artificial settings that are far removed from the natural environment of the customer, where his or her experiences with the product or company take place. As a result, customers are asked to remember or imagine, but both thought processes are subject to all sorts of distortions. What is needed, therefore, to do relevant experiential research is to conduct it in the customer's natural environment. Moreover, experiences are extended over time. They are not one-shot impressions but happen over the course of a shopping trip, during an interaction with service personnel, as part of an online session, and so on. As we are observing customers in their natural environment, we need to follow them around while they immerse themselves in the experience and ask them about what they like, what they don't like, and what they would like to change.

2. *Use realistic stimuli to elicit relevant customer responses.* Most stimuli shown in traditional research (products, Web sites, and shopping environments) are impoverished representations of the actual stimuli customers receive. Researchers often describe products instead of showing them; Web sites are presented as graphical mock-ups; shopping environments are exhibited in photos. Realistic three-dimensional, multisensory, and multimedia displays and mock-up environments are missing. We need to use

such displays and environments in experiential research to elicit relevant customer responses.

3. *Encourage customers to imagine a different reality.* Most research focuses on the status quo and asks the customer to describe or react to what is currently available. However, the objective of a CEM project is usually to look into the future, and to launch a new brand experience, restructure the interface, or engage in innovation. Therefore, we want customers to think about future desirable experiences as well as to evaluate present ones. Not only do they need to critique what is now; they also need to help us create what is next and imagine the future. Thus, research must serve not only as an assessment but also as the creative voice of the customer. We need to encourage customers to become aware of assumptions, at times override them, and get them to imagine a different reality.

In sum, experiential research needs to occur, whenever possible, in the customer's natural environment; we need to ask customers to respond to realistic stimuli that successfully simulate the real world, and we need to encourage them to look into the future and imagine a different reality.

How can managers do all this? Here are some techniques.

Observing Customers in Their Natural Habitat

In *Body Ritual among the Nacirema,* author Horace Miner provided an ethnographic account of the taboos and ceremonial behaviors among the members of a magic-ridden society. Here is a short excerpt about the culture's body ritual.[2] See if you can guess the culture:

> The fundamental belief underlying the whole system appears to be that the human body is ugly and that its natural tendency is to debility and disease. Incarcerated in such a body, man's only hope is to avert these characteristics through the use of ritual and ceremony. Every household has one or more shrines devoted to this purpose. The more powerful individuals in the society have several shrines in their houses and, in fact, the opulence of a house is often referred to in terms of the number of such ritual centers it possesses. Most houses are of wattle and daub construction, but the shrine rooms of the more wealthy are walled with stone. Poorer families imitate the rich by applying pottery plaques to their shrine wall.

Congratulations. You got it. "Nacirema" is "American" spelled backward, and Miner was demonstrating what happens when you take an anthropological approach to something that you normally take for granted. The "shrines" he describes are the bathrooms we all consider a perfectly normal part of our lives.

Today's experiential marketers are following in Miner's footsteps by taking an anthropological perspective on consumers to see how they behave in their "natural habitat." Researchers spend time with consumers in their homes, observing them as they use products, and interviewing them for their impressions of these products. For example, as described in an article in the New York Times, researchers observe a woman taking a shower and using various soap products. "My ex-husband showed up last Friday," explains the woman. "I got so stressed out that I had to take a shower immediately." Taking notes, the researcher in-quires, "How does the Softsoap compare with the Oil of Olay?" "Well, the Softsoap foams up better," observes the woman. "I like the pump on it. I definitely like pumping better than squirt-ing. I like the control of the pump." "So," the researcher probes, "you think the pump is a kind of control mechanism?"

Over the top? Maybe, but this kind of research is providing marketers with valuable information essential to understand-ing today's consumers.

The experiential research on the concert-going experience at Carnegie Hall described earlier also falls into this "natural habi-tat research" category. Participants were actually attending a performance, not just remembering one or evaluating the orga-nization in the abstract. As a result, they could respond directly to what they heard, saw, and felt at the performance.

Using Realistic Stimuli

For stimuli to be realistic, we need to make sure that they are similar to the often multisensory and multimedia, three-dimensional stimuli that customers receive in their daily lives. With today's technologies, this has become a realistic goal, and I am at times amazed with the artificial and contrived stimuli presentations that some research firms still get away with.

As part of a project for a cosmetics firm, we made sure that customers received realistic stimuli at every stage of the project. We conducted an observational study—an ethnography of the brand—by observing and following the customer around while shopping for and using the brand. Moreover, we performed qualitative and quantitative research on the experiential world

81

FIGURE 3.9

Three dimensional, multi-sensory display board used in research for Laneige brand. *Credit:* Courtesy of AmorePacific.

of the customer using three dimensional multisensory display boards and videos that were constructed in collaboration with a graphic design firm specializing in consumer trends. Moreover, we examined the competition by taking a close look at the imagery they used. In later phases of the project, target customers were shown visual boards of potential experiential platforms and of implementations in packaging and sales promotions. I highly recommend that you use similar techniques in your own experiential projects.

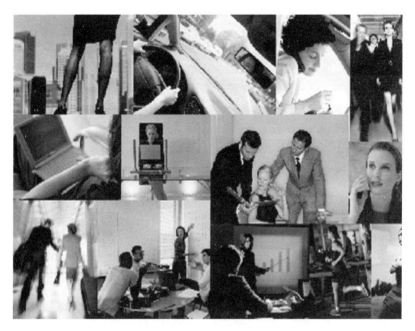

FIGURE 3.10

Images used in video about customer lifestyle for Laneige brand. *Credit:* Courtesy of AmorePacific.

Examining the Future

One way to examine the future is to work closely with experts and to examine expert media because they are often ahead of the curve. Using a diverse group of experts (Levi's calls them "trend scouts") and/or expert media is often instructive. In the cosmetics project, we conducted focus groups with fashion and beauty editors of fashion and lifestyle magazines and con-tent-analyzed fashion, lifestyle, home living, and technology magazines. Another great source of inspiration, especially for lifestyle trends, is usually the street (the "cool street," not Wall Street).

If the project is less focused on imagery and communications and more on new product development, it is a good idea to work with expert users. To provide top-quality athletic footwear, Nike employs sports specialists who work closely with athletes and coaches to perfect the shoe and the experience with it. These specialists are experts in human biomechanics (i.e., in applying their knowledge of mechanics to the human body). They conduct in-depth research in the Nike Sports Research Laboratory studying the game, fine-tuning their understanding of the athlete's needs, and anticipating developments in the marketplace. They develop innovations based on close and detailed observations of athletes' desired experiences for performance and comfort.

The way a given player plays the game can change the requirement for the shoe. In basketball, the power center is a big player—close to seven feet tall and weighing 250 to 275 pounds—running up and down the court at a leisurely pace compared with the other players. Observations reveal that he spends about 40 percent of the time under the hoop pushing in a defensive or offensive position. For another 40 percent he stands around with his arms in the air. This player therefore requires a great deal of protection because of the jumping and because of his size. In contrast, a guard who is only six feet five inches and weighs considerably less (say, 180 pounds), is sprinting—accelerating and slowing down—and is not at a constant speed. He experiences a lot of shear force motion compared with the power center whose motion is up and down. As a result, the guard needs a different shoe from the center.

Nike gains further insights when athletes are testing shoes in development. Athletes are involved either in one-on-one situations or as part of focus groups with designers and engineers. Nike has more than 5,000 registered testers in the United States, as well as high school and college teams and elite players in Europe and Asia.

The problem with experts can be that they refuse to think out of the box. That is why it is important to use a diverse group and bring them together in a natural setting. With its current technique, Nike may get a great performing shoe. But will it be a fashion item? Perhaps they don't want it to be one (like Puma; see Chapter 4)—but if they did, an inspiring technique might be to bring together fashion designers and athletes—and perhaps sculptors and graphic artists.

Conclusion

Understanding the experiential world of the customer is the first step in a CEM project. To do so, you need to identify the target customer for the experience, divide the experiential world into four layers, track the experience along touchpoints, and survey the competitive landscape. Most important, you need to use original and creative research techniques to provide true customer insight. At this point you are ready to begin building the experiential platform, which we will discuss next.

Building the Experiential Platform

An important part of business and marketing strategy is what managers call "positioning"—how the company wants customers to perceive the organization, its brands, and its products. In most companies, however, positioning consists of a vague and sometimes pompous internally focused statement that penetrates the organization only as far as the sheets of the strategy report. Moreover, nobody takes implementing the statement seriously because it contains almost no information about how to accomplish that task.

The CEM framework, on the other hand, uses a customer-oriented, dynamic concept—the *experiential platform*—to articulate the positioning of a company, brand, or product. The experiential platform provides the strategic connection between analysis and implementation. It uses the insights about the customer's experiential world derived from the in-depth analysis in the prior CEM step. The platform forms the basis for the subsequent three implementation steps (the brand experience, the customer interface, and innovations). In contrast to traditional positioning, the experiential platform effectively communicates internally and externally what an organization, its brand, and its products stand for and what value they offer to customers. Managers can use this information to structure and coordinate implementation programs.

This chapter covers the benefits and strategy components of an experiential platform—*experiential positioning*, the *experiential value promise*, and the *overall implementation theme*. You can use the first component, experiential positioning, to depict what the brand stands for; in the second component, the experiential value promise, you specify what the customer gets; with the third component, you link the positioning and value promise to actual implementation. You lay out the style and content that govern all implementations.

The following two examples illustrate what an experiential platform is and what it does. Jamba Juice is a California-based fruit juice and smoothies company that, since the mid-1990s, has been very successful with its outlets in that state and other parts of the United States. Cingular, a wireless carrier, started services in the United States in 2001.

Jamba Juice: A Platform of Fun and Good Health

Jamba Juice, a privately held company, was founded in 1990 under the name of *Juice Club* stores by four young entrepreneurs in San Luis Obispo, California. Since Jamba Juice's beginning, there has been an increase in the country's nutritional awareness and the company has swept across the country quenching customers' thirst with an unparalleled sensory experience.

Jamba Juice has become the category-defining leader in all-natural, made-to-order fruit smoothies, juices, and healthy snacks. The company maintains its reputation by offering a daily ritual that provides a healthy boost through made-to-order products, prepared with wholesome ingredients, in a vibrant environment by passionate people who care.

The term "Jamba" means to celebrate, and that's the core of Jamba Juice's experiential positioning: "every time we take your order, we make our blenders dance, and put the party in your cup—along with a straw tested for its 'suckability factor.' "

The company promises to use only the highest quality ingredients and no artificial preservatives, flavors, or colors. But there is more to it. The company's experiential value promise also includes a broader concern for health and the environment. For example, at Jamba Juice the drink is served in a styrofoam cup that is recyclable and environmentally safe to produce. As an alternative, customers can buy a plastic cup that they can re-use again and again.

Despite its serious concern for health and the environment, though, Jamba Juice does not come across too seriously. Instead, every aspect of the implementation is in line with creativity and fun.

For example, Jamba Juice products have unique names and descriptions, in addition to the more serious listings of the product ingredients and nutrition facts. Consider the following names for its smoothies and fruit drinks:

- Coldbuster, a smoothie that "combats colds with 2,100% D.V. of Vitamin C and Echinacea."
- Protein Berry Pizzazz, "packed with over 20 grams of protein for muscle maintenance and sustained energy."
- Kiwi Berry Burner, which "promotes weight maintenance with chromium and other botanicals."

The natural ingredients in Jamba smoothies can be complemented with Jamba "boosts." Jamba Boosts are high-quality, effective, uniquely blended vitamin, mineral, and herb supplements to boost body and mind. Jamba offers nine Boosts including favorites like:

- Vita Boost for "total, vital health [that] nourishes the whole body with 100% RDI of 20 vitamins and minerals."
- Femme Boost is "designed specifically for women [to] help balance, protect, and support the body's needs with 100% RDI of vitamin A and D, folic acid, calcium, and magnesium, plus iron, botanicals, and herbs like wild yam, and chasteberry."
- Energy Boost for "mind and body energy" has been developed to "stimulate body and mind, fight fatigue, and increase stamina with Siberian Ginseng, Gingko Biloba, and other energy-producing vitamins and minerals."

In addition to the smoothies and boosts, Jamba Juice also serves fresh squeezed juices, nutritious soups, and snacks like breads and pretzels. The store atmosphere is fun and playful. Above the counters is a colorful and funky menu with images

FIGURE 4.1
Interior of Jamba Juice store. Photo courtesy of Jamba Juice.

of fruits and veggies. Jamba Juice team members are passionate about what they do and enjoy working with their customers in the vibrant atmosphere created in each Jamba location.

As part of its quality control, the company pays attention to the little details such as the "suckability factor" of the straw. To ensure the consistency of its experiential platform, the company

FIGURE 4.2

Jamba Juice store display featuring energy-boosting wheat grass. Photo courtesy of Jamba Juice.

has only a very limited franchise program, primarily including licenses for companies and institutions that control institutional sites like universities and airports. There are no individual franchises to the general public.

The customer feedback questionnaire can tell you a lot about a how a company sees itself and what it values. In the case of Jamba Juice, the Comment Card indicates clearly that the company's platform is focused on experience and shows how it intends to implement this platform. The Comment Card, which every customer who visits a Jamba Juice store can complete, asks the customer to "share your Jamba experience with us," and the first question asks for a rating of the "overall experience." Other items indicate what the company seems to value in its store: a sincere greeting, team member appearance, taste and consistency, teamwork and overall energy, speed and a sense of urgency, cleanliness, and organization, a sincere "thank you" or salutation, and the right music level. Jamba Juice receives more than 800 e-mails and letters daily plus additional 4,000 to 6,000 comment cards each month, all of which are closely monitored and responded to by a team member.

So far, Jamba Juice has always received high marks from me. Whenever I'm in Los Angeles, I make sure I live Southern-California style for a day or two, and Jamba Juice is part of my daily routine. I ask my colleagues and friends to drive huge distances just to have a smoothie early in the morning right after the store opens, and often another one at night. For me and many other customers, Jamba provides just the rightexperience.

Cingular Wireless: Humanizing the Wireless Experience

An amalgam of Southwestern Bell and Bell South wireless companies, Cingular began operations in January 2001 with the goal of "redefining communications according to humanity, not technology." Entering the market during a time of confusion and dissatisfaction with telecommunication services, Cingular seized this opportunity to redefine the customer wireless experience. The only major player that is exclusively wireless, Cingular defined its experiential platform thus:

> Cingular exists to serve the innate human need to be heard and recognized by enhancing the human tools of expression, not by replacing them. Cingular is not technology. It does not create the need to communicate. Cingular exists to enhance

the human voice, the human hand, the human ear, the human eye—all to give people the opportunity to shout and be heard, to listen and be educated, to recognize and be recognized.

According to its Web site:

[Cingular] is dedicated to self-expression and customer-friendly service. . . . A leader in mobile voice and data communications, Cingular is a wireless company determined to promote the individual to a new level and to create a personal relationship with each of its customers. . . . Cingular's vision is to simplify the wireless experience for its consumer and business customers by offering easy-to-understand, affordable rate plans and excellent customer service.

FIGURE 4.3

Cingular Wireless print ad. *Credit:* Courtesy of BBDO advertising agency.

FIGURE 4.4

Cingular Wireless print ad for New York market. *Credit:* Courtesy of BBDO advertising agency. Photography by Darrin Hadad.

To deliver its experiential platform, Cingular created a character, or icon, a stylized *x* shape with a dot for a "head," suggesting the human form—an ideal symbol for Cingular's commitment to "humanity." More flexible than a logo, it can be animated and it "speaks." The icon is the star of Cingular's playful ad campaign, in which it declares: "You better believe this new company believes in self-expression. Look at me. I'm naked." And "Life isn't a library. You're allowed to talk." Some are downright silly, serving more to call attention to the company and its spirit than to advertise its platform or services. One print ad depicts the head of the icon as a baseball smashing a window.

Another shows the icon looking up at an x-shaped lug wrench and wondering "mom?"

Cingular's approach has been remarkably successful. In only four months, it achieved 59 percent brand awareness in its initial target market area. As of this writing, Cingular Wireless is the second largest wireless company in the United States, and growing.

In the summer of 2002, Cingular launched a big push into Northeast markets, especially New York City. "Nobody knows self-expression like New Yorkers, and Cingular is empowering citizens of the Big Apple with world-class wireless voices and data services to express themselves like never before," said Stephen Carter, president and CEO of Cingular.

As part of the push, the company opened a creative "experiential space" in Rockefeller Center. I visited the new Cingular Zone and found a variety of activities linked to Cingular's experiential platform of human self-expression. At the center of the Zone is the Live Bar, where visitors can make a free wireless phone call anywhere in the United States; then on a huge map of the country, they can place a special marker at the location they called. The Cingular character was also present, in the "Express Yourself" station, where visitors can decorate their own version of the icon. Visitors are also invited to step up onto a literal experiential platform—a stage with a backdrop of the New York skyline and express themselves on the theme, "Why I Love New York." Everyone gets a CD or DVD of their performance; the best performances are shown and replayed on the Zone's video screens and may appear in upcoming Cingular ads. Cingular also sponsored an artwork installation by video and laser artist Nam June Paik at Rockefeller Center as its summer

2002 art spectacular. The laser work called "Transmission" was modeled after a 1930s-era radio tower and sent red, green, and blue laser beams from the tip of its 33-foot tower from dusk until midnight, drawing millions of visitors.

Benefits of the Experiential Platform

Jamba Juice and Cingular demonstrate how a well-developed experiential platform can provide a blueprint for every touchpoint between the company and its customers.

Building an experiential platform has several managerial benefits: first, it captures insight about customers because it is developed out of their experiential world; second, it provides coordination; and third, it is specific and thus an excellent sketch for implementation.

Let's look at each benefit.

First, the experiential platform springs directly from the experiential world of the customer. At times, knowledge about the customer is largely intuitive. Especially in the case of a start-up company, the founders may have a gut feeling that the time is right for their idea and product. The same gut instinct and desire to change the world exists not only in business-to-consumer markets but also in the business-to-business world. SAP is one of the largest software companies in the world. It was founded in the mid-1980s by two ex-IBM engineers, Hasso Plattner and Dietmar Hopp, who understood that large enterprises needed software that could integrate business processes such as inventory planning, supply management, financial planning, and sales forecasts. Thus, the enterprise resource software movement was born.

However, the experiential platform does not have to rely just on instinct. As we'll see in this chapter, you can use a systematic methodology and research techniques to develop and fine-tune an experiential platform for business success. Then, the experiential platform incorporates relevant knowledge and insight based on qualitative and quantitative research of the experiential world of the customer.

The second major benefit of building an experiential platform is that it provides coordination by connecting key internal personnel with external firms involved in the implementation. Because the platform provides coordination, it may even eliminate the need to bring in other firms. Once key players in the organization understand the experiential platform, it can provide tangible guidance that reaches far beyond the usual strategy statements. This knowledge enables internal employees to do some of the creative work previously farmed out to other companies.

At Calvin Klein, the upscale fashion company run by Mr. Klein himself, advertising and communications are done in-house without an external ad agency. Klein often is personally involved in developing and expressing the provocative, and at times outrageous, platform of the company. From a 15-year-old Brooke Shields claiming that nothing came between her and her Calvins to sexy photos for its underwear line, Calvin Klein advertising has always attracted attention. "It always seems to me that it would be more pure, direct, honest, and simple to be involved in that process myself. It's an extension of creation. So, little by little, I started working with art directors, creative directors, photographers, stylists, all kinds of creative people. We always looked at it as just fun. But there's clearly a

97

message with all of the various campaigns that we've done. It really communicates. It just shocks you. I'm great at taking risks, and these things get noticed."[1]

A third major benefit of the experiential platform is that it is specific and linked to implementation. It thus goes far beyond traditional strategy, positioning statements, and value-proposition formulations, which are often generic and difficult to relate to customers' daily experiences. The methodologies and research techniques used for formulating the experiential platform are based on multidimensional verbal and visual insights about customers and can be used easily to design the brand experience, structure the customer interface, and engage in continuous innovation.

The Strategy Components of the Experiential Platform

As shown in Figure 4.5, the experiential platform consists of three strategy components: the *experiential positioning*, the *experiential value promise (EVP)*, and the *overall implementation theme*.

1. The experiential positioning depicts what the brand stands for. It is equivalent to the positioning statement of traditional management and marketing, but it replaces that vague positioning statement with an insightful and useful multisensory strategy component that is full of imagery and relevant to the buyers and users of the brand.

2. The EVP describes, in experiential terms, what the customer gets. It is the experiential equivalent to the

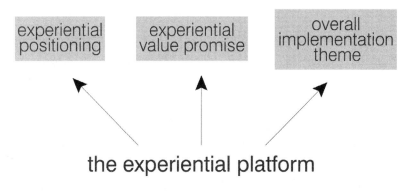

FIGURE 4.5
CEM's Experiential Platform: Three Strategy Components

functional value proposition, which is often trite and commonplace because it focuses solely on functional product attributes and benefits. The EVP identifies in experiential terms the *specific* value the customer can expect from the brand.

3. The overall implementation theme summarizes the style and content of the core messages that the company will use across all implementations in the brand experience, the customer interface, and future innovations.

Experiential Positioning

The experiential positioning is an image-driven depiction of the experience that the brand stands for. For Jamba Juice, the experiential positioning is a fun, health experience. For Cingular, it is human self-expression.

The experiential positioning should be tangible enough that we immediately know what to do with it. At the same time, it should be intriguing so we can launch innovative implementations. From an organizational perspective, it helps when the experiential positioning stretches employees' imagination.

At times, a company needs to update the experiential platform. When a company enters a new market, the platform may need to be localized a bit. The experiential positioning may need to change entirely under certain dramatic changes in the world of the customer.

The terrorist attacks of September 11, 2001, proved to be such an event. Marketing research, through consumer surveys and focus groups, indicated that after the attacks people wanted to live with more community focus, truth, authenticity, loyalty, honesty, and sincerity. The end-of-the-century and turn-of-the-millennium extravaganza and the widespread sense of omnipotence abruptly seemed to be "off-trend." Accordingly, experiential positioning in the post-9/11 world included these emerging themes.

This shift in values was apparent almost immediately in the art and fashion world. Whimsical and playful images, reminiscent of the pop art movement in the 1960s, dominated art, fashion, and advertising graphics. Christian Dior, which had been running a controversial campaign showing models with dirt on their bodies and in some ads even looking as if they had been beaten or harassed, was suddenly all smiles. Louis Vuitton changed its high-tech, fast-paced advertisements to images from fairy tales, such as a fashion-victim Sleeping Beauty with a red apple (and LV bag) lying beside her, or Snow White, with her dwarfs, in a contemporary yet dreamy white outfit. In other industries, too, communications got more dreamlike, soft, and communal.

In addition to responding to changes in the environment, a company's experiential positioning needs to be integrated through organizational alignment and communicated to the customer. Such organizational alignment might start with a public statement by the company that it is committed to de-livering a certain experience for their customers—at every touchpoint.

Delta Airlines has started such an initiative. The company published a 12-point "Customer Commitment" statement about what customers can expect before their flight, at the air-port, and after landing. Delta's commitments include:

- Offering on the phone the lowest fare for which the cus-tomer is eligible for the date, flight, and class of service re-quested, and making the customer aware that lower fares may be available on the Web.
- Holding reservations without payment until midnight one day after the reservation was made.
- Refunding tickets within seven days for credit card purchases.
- Providing full and timely information on the status of de-layed and canceled flights.
- Attempting to return misplaced baggage within 24 hours.
- Responding to customer complaints within 30 days.

Delta's effort at developing this customer commitment initia-tive should be applauded. The promise is incomplete, however, and in many cases does not go far enough. For example, several commitments are industry-standard and hardly differentiate the airline from its competitors. Moreover, the "in-flight experience" is not mentioned among the customer commitments, perhaps because promises about people are more difficult to deliver on than promises that require databases and technology. This omission is understandable, but isn't the inflight experience the most important and relevant aspect of the customer contact for an airline?

A customer commitment has to be achievable; that is, the company needs to have the technology and human resources to deliver it consistently. At the same time, it must differentiate the company and focus on the relevant aspects of the customer experience.

The EVP

A value proposition is a core part of any customer strategy. All too often, however, it is a purely functional statement of what the customers get for their money. In contrast, the *experiential value promise* (EVP) specifies precisely what the experiential positioning will do for the customer: it states what the customer will "get" as an experience; the company must fulfill this promise, or the customer will be disappointed.

For many years, Nike's EVP has been to provide functionally superior shoes and sportswear that will allow customers to engage in superior performance. That is what Nike promises and guarantees to its customers.

Nike's EVP, along with everything the company does, reflects this. In implementing the brand experience, Nike's emphasis is on product functionality (the shoe must fit, perform, and protect). The company's Web site provides detailed information about the technology related to the performance characteristics of the shoe. In addition, as noted in Chapter 3, Nike's product development focuses on a detailed understanding of the athlete's requirements for a high-performance shoe.

The EVP of Puma, a successful Nike competitor, is different. Puma's product line includes labels like "Roller Kitty," "Platinum," and "Icana." Puma wants to be "the brand that mixes the influences of sports, lifestyle, and fashion. . . . Puma makes products designed to facilitate the individual achievements that evoke the most passionate responses." Note the language and how the value promised to the Puma customer differs from Nike's EVP: "mixes the influences," "lifestyle and fashion," "passionate responses."

FIGURE 4.6

Puma print ad: tennis celebrity Serena Williams. *Credit:* Courtsey of Puma North America.

Appropriately, to provide lifestyle and fashion values and passionate responses, Puma has collaborated with Xuly Bet, AEROSPACE, German fashion designer Jil Sander, and, recently, Japanese designer Yasuhiro Mihara. The lifestyle and fitness-inspired shoes—which are available at high-end boutiques and department stores in the United States, France, Germany, Italy, Japan, and the United Kingdom—come in such colors as gray/camel, wine/purple, yellow/apricot, and violet/tan.

The choice of EVP can determine tangible outcomes such as sales, market share, and profitability. Consider the athletic shoe market one more time and the consequences of alternative EVPs for Nike and Puma. Will consumers of the future seek value in performance-driven or in lifestyle and fashion-influenced athletic shoes? How often will consumers want to replace them? How will each type of shoe be priced? Answers to these

FIGURE 4.7

Puma print ad: skateboarding champ Kien Lu. *Credit:* Courtesy of Puma North America.

questions will depend on how consumers think about and experience athletic shoes in the future. Consumers may ask, "How much performance innovation can there really be in this market?" "How much performance do I need?" "How much am I willing to pay for it?" "Should an athletic shoe be a fashion statement?" "Can performance and fashion go together?" Assume that there is a desire or a segment for both types of shoes or shoe occasions: performance and fashion. Then the outcome of the game will depend on how well a company like Nike can persuade customers that they need a different shoe for every sport, and how well companies like Puma can persuade customers that they should wear fashion-inspired shoes for many kinds of occasions. In addition, it will depend on the replacement cycle of the shoes (is it likely to be shorter for performance because of wear-out or new technologies, or for fashion because of changing styles?) and on the price a customer is willing to pay.

In specifying the EVP, it is often useful to think in terms of the types of experiences I discussed in my prior book, *Experiential Marketing*. They include sensory experiences (*sense*); affective experiences (*feel*); cognitive experiences (*think*); physical experiences, behaviors, and lifestyles (*act*); and social-identity experiences that result from relating to a reference group or culture (*relate*).

- The sense experience appeals to the five senses; customer value is created through sight, sound, touch, taste, and smell.

- The feel experience appeals to customers' inner feelings and emotions; customer value is created through affective experiences that range from mildly positive moods linked to a

105

brand (e.g., for a noninvolving, nondurable grocery brand or service, or industrial product) to strong emotions of joy and pride (e.g., for a consumer durable, technology, or social marketing campaign).

- The think experience appeals to the intellect; it creates value for customers by engaging them creatively.

- The act experience appeals to behaviors and lifestyles, creating value for customers by showing them alternative lifestyles or alternative ways of doing business (e.g., in business-to-business and industrial markets).

- The relate experience contains social experiences. It creates value for the customer by providing a social identity and sense of belonging.

Rarely do CEM projects result in only one type of experience. Many successful CEM projects employ experiential hybrids that produce several experiences. Ideally, management should strive strategically to create holistic experiences that possess, at the same time, sense, feel, think, act, and relate qualities.

A 2002 campaign for Kraft's Life Savers, the number-one nonchocolate candy brand, provided a holistic experience. The campaign focused on candy-flavor personalities (e.g., Ms. Popularity for cherry; the Runner-Up for orange; the Old Timer for butter rum; the Quiet Type for pineapple). The campaign had sensory appeal, made consumers feel good and engaged their thinking; moreover, the candy personalities had lifestyle and relational appeal.

The EVP, in conjunction with the experiential positioning, will guide marketing and management actions toward

Box 4.1

TYPES OF EXPERIENCE AND LIKELIHOOD OF PURCHASE

Are customers more likely to buy a product that simultaneously triggers several types of experience compared with a product that triggers only one?

This question was addressed in the research on the impact of experiences on customer impressions, attitudes, and purchase intention (see Chapter 1). The figure below shows the relationship between the number of activated experiences and purchase intention. When no experience was activated (because the product or communication was entirely functional), purchase intention was 58 percent. Purchase intention went up to 67 percent for one experience and to 77 percent for three or more types of experience—an increase of more than one third! The data shows the value of striving for hybrid and holistic experiences.

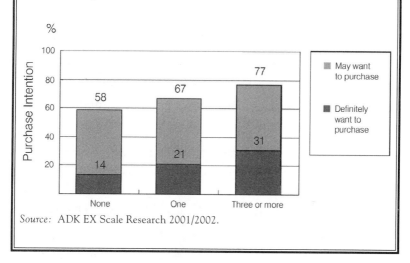

Source: ADK EX Scale Research 2001/2002.

customers. Moreover, the EVP can help managers develop innovative ventures and initiatives. As shown in the athletic shoes example, the EVP can even provide critical input for financial expectations, thus linking customer experience with customer equity. This relationship between customer experience and customer equity is explored further in Chapter 9.

The Overall Implementation Theme

The experiential platform for the brand culminates in an *overall implementation theme*. This theme is a concrete manifestation of the platform—a value-adding concept that can be implemented in the style and content of the brand, interface, and innovation elements.

The overall theme is important not only to provide input for the implementation elements but also to sequence them. Imagine you are launching a new brand in an existing market or entering a new market with an existing brand that requires localization, or both. In 2002, I was involved in a situation that was new on both dimensions: a company had to launch a new brand in a market that was new to the firm and of key strategic importance. The company had come up with an overall implementation theme that it needed to put in place. A key issue was the right mix and sequencing of standard advertising with less conventional forms of marketing communications (e.g., buzz and guerrilla marketing). The theme included experiences as they relate to certain holidays and seasons ("The December Holiday Season is a time of sharing," "Summer is the time of freshness and outdoors," etc.) and provided valuable guidance for timing these different forms of marketing and communication initiatives.

Red Bull, an energy drink, is an example of a successful implementation theme. Red Bull is popular among the club-hopping youth (and those who want to feel young) in Europe and the United States. The drink contains caffeine and amino acids such as taurine (thus the word "bull" in the product's name) and glucuronolacine. Taurine acts as a metabolic transmitter that has a detoxifying effect that strengthens cardiac contractility; glucuronolacine helps eliminate harmful substances and accelerates metabolism. Launched in 1987 by Dietrich Mateschutz in Austria, Red Bull sold 1 million cans in its first year and around 1 billion cans in 2000.

This exponential growth came about not only because of the unusual ingredients of the drink, but because of a focused experiential platform. Red Bull's experiential positioning is "energy in a bottle"; its EVP is "strengthening the heart, accelerating the metabolism, and fighting stress." The implementation theme is centered on staying fit for all sorts of social fun activities: for the clubbing crowd worldwide, drinking Red Bull is like injecting a dose of energy and stamina that helps them move faster and faster to the escalating beats of electronic and trance music.

Red Bull has taken a creative approach in delivering its overall implementation theme through a set of initiatives such as the Red Bull Music Academy, the Red Bull Acro team, and the Red Bull Yamaha and Junior teams. The Red Bull Music Academy is particularly interesting because the company created it for the exploration of music history, technology, and business. The purpose of this project is to offer a forum where enthusiasts from all over the world can share music, ideas, and knowledge. Selected applicants have participated in two-part workshops that were held in Berlin in 1998 and 1999, Dublin in 2000, New York in 2001, and London in 2002. Participants are DJ's with good music and a passion for producing, who listen to well-known guest speakers, and DJ's from the underground club scene. This project particularly reinforces Red Bull's association with raves and electronic music while creating an ideal environment for the product's consumption.

Researching and Presenting the Experiential Platform

Just as there are methodologies and research techniques for understanding the experiential world of the customer, similar methodologies and techniques are helpful for building the experiential platform. As you recall, in the context of the experiential world, these methodologies and techniques focus on exploration and idea-generation. For the experiential platform, the focus is on testing strategy options.

The methodology for arriving at an experiential platform consists of the following three steps:

1. *Choose an experiential positioning.* The key input here is the outcome of research about the customer.

A project that I conducted for a skin care and cosmetics brand illustrates this step. The analysis of the customer's experiential world had resulted in the selection of "naturalism" as a key trend that was relevant for fashion, lifestyles and, most important, cosmetics. Naturalism had tested very well in qualitative and quantitative research and was seen as an interesting option for further study. Several new product and communication options for the brand had also been suggested in the experiential world analysis. Thus, to test strategy options both verbally and visually as well as to select an experiential positioning, we first conducted a conceptual analysis and empirical research with hundreds of consumers. It was found that naturalism had three experiential positioning options: first, naturalism in terms of natural ingredients of cosmetics; second, naturalism in terms of a natural look; third, naturalism in terms of natural behavior toward others. Results of the testing favored an experiential positioning that combined the second and third options: the "outer and inner beauty" of a contemporary, joyful young woman.

2. *Specify an experiential value promise.* As discussed earlier, the EVP should be formulated in terms of its sense, feel, think, act, and relate impact on consumers. You can test whether these aspects of an experience provide value with a measurement scale that I designed for different aspects of the experience. Applying the scale in the cosmetics project, we found out that the experiential positioning provided value in terms of sense (beauty and youth), feel (joy), think (the intriguing idea of outer and inner beauty), and act (using cosmetics that are youthful and allow a woman to behave accordingly).

3. *Create an overall implementation theme.* With such a theme requires analytical thinking and creativity. Subsequently, managers can test the theme in ad concept testing, in design concept testing, and as a potential viable option for the interface and innovations.

FIGURE 4.8

From top left to bottom right: web site, store bags, ad story board, product line of Laneige brand. *Credit:* Courtesy of AmorePacific.

In the skin care and cosmetics brand project, the final implementation theme, developed out of the EVP, was "light and water." The overall implementation theme was displayed and communicated in the form of a concept theme video, including key verbal content (buzz words and messages that express the theme) and prototypical imagery (photos and other images). This theme was shared within the organization and external firms and then implemented in an original way in the brand experience and the customer interface, and it resulted in new product development and innovation (see Figure 4.8).

Conclusion

Formulating an experiential platform is the key strategy step of a CEM project. In this step, we use our understanding of the experiential world of the customers to formulate an experiential positioning, a value promise for them, and an overall implementation theme. The experiential platform is communicated through verbal and visual imagery associated with the company and its brands. An experience video can be used to communicate the overall implementation theme to relevant constituents of the organization and external firms that work with the firm. Once we have done the analytical, strategic, and creative work of this step, we are ready to implement the experience in all forms of brand communications and the pertinent interface, and we can use the platform to drive innovation. Chapters 5 through 7 cover these topics.

Box 4.2

JETBLUE: AN UNEXPECTED EXPERIENCE

When JetBlue Airways began service on February 11, 2000, it knew exactly what it wanted to be: a cheap airline with a unique experience for the smart hip crowd. Described as a cross between Southwest Airlines and Virgin Atlantic, JetBlue provides travelers with an inexpensive, no-frills, high-quality experience in the air. Inexpensive, no-frills, *and* high quality? Let's take a closer look at this unexpected combination.

(continued)

Box 4.2 Continued

Although JetBlue has early bookings at comparable fares to competitors, JetBlue almost always beats the competition for flights booked one or two days before travel dates. Fares are low. All seats are assigned, all travel is ticketless, all fares are one-way, and a Saturday night stay is never required. Booking is straightforward and simple, with no games and no bizarre fare structures.

Being a no-frills airline, JetBlue provides minimal in-flight service and does not serve meals. But the in-flight experience is not disappointing. On the contrary, every seat on JetBlue is equipped with complimentary Live TV offering 24 channels of DIRECTV programming. What's more, you will never miss that microwaved whatever-it-is; instead, JetBlue gives out high-quality snacks like Terra potato chips. Don't

Courtesy of JetBlue Airways.

Box 4.2 Continued

look for that cheap, threadbare orange upholstery, either; all the seats on JetBlue are leather. JetBlue has 36 new Airbus A320s and is in the process of adding more, providing travelers with a clean and quiet ride.

JetBlue's attention to the customer experience starts at the top. The company's founder and CEO David Neeleman makes it a point to ride on a JetBlue flight almost every week. While on board, he helps the flight attendants serve snacks, but his main activity is to listen to his customers—what they like, what they dislike, what changes they'd like to see. He's listening for big ideas—"why don't you expand the number of cities you serve?"—and for little ones—"why

Courtesy of JetBlue Airways.

(continued)

Box 4.2   Continued

don't you show fewer sports shows on the video?" He gets ideas and runs them by his customers. For example, would women passengers prefer a women-only lavatory? Neeleman is so obsessed with being inside the customer experience that he carries a pager day and night, with instructions that he be paged any time a JetBlue flight is more than one minute late.

Neeleman's approach to building this customer-friendly airline is something any businessperson can emulate: he worked from his own experience and that of the people around him. The leather seats, for example, were his idea. After having been seated in a urine-soaked seat on a different airline, Neeleman understood that the leather seating was worth the additional cost in the comfort it gave his passengers.

David Neeleman started the airline with the aspiration of bringing "humanity back to air travel." By all indications, he is succeeding. JetBlue was voted the country's number-two domestic airline in the *Condé Nast Traveler* 14th Annual Readers' Choice Awards. JetBlue also received the highest score of any airline in the *Condé Nast Traveler* 2001 Business Travel Awards (it was the number one U.S. airline in the coach-only category). Most important, JetBlue posted U.S.$26.8 million in operating profit in 2001, compared with the U.S.$10 billion in losses by other airlines in the same period.

Not your typical cut-rate airline. As JetBlue's success demonstrates, pay attention to the customer experience and the sky's the limit.*

---

*Melanie Wells, "Lord of the Skies," *Forbes* (October 14, 2002), p. 130ff, and Internet sources.

Designing the Brand Experience

In Chapter 4, you learned how to build an experiential platform that serves as a bridge between analysis and implementation. In the following three chapters, we turn to the concepts and methodologies for implementing the brand experience, the customer interface, and continuous innovation.

In this chapter, we focus on *the brand experience*. It includes all the static elements that the customer encounters—the product itself, logos and signage, packaging, brochures, and advertising. These elements are static in the sense that the company produces them (in its factory or marketing department) or outsources them to external firms (corporate identity firms, graphic designers, and advertising agencies). They are then delivered to the customer in this predesigned state.

The brand experience is not dynamic or customized: it is not created in a real-time interaction with the customer (as may happen during a service encounter or a telephone interaction, a sales call, or through an interactive encounter on the Web). The dynamic customer interface is covered in Chapter 6.

Some situations, such as a store visit, involve the customer in both a static brand experience and an interactive interface experience. In the store, the customer encounters many static elements that are part of the brand experience (the architectural/interior design, store decorations, ad panels, etc.), as well as dynamic elements that are part of the customer interface (interaction with salespeople and service staff). The Web experience is another mixed situation. Any Web site will have static graphic designs, but usually there are also dynamic, interactive elements (searches, company contacts, e-commerce features, and chat rooms).

Planning and designing the brand experience requires that we use the overall implementation theme of the experiential platform. The customer encounters the brand experience in direct experience with the product, in its look and feel (e.g., on bottles, containers, boxes, or other forms of packaging), in commercially produced communications (brochures, print and TV advertising, Web design, etc.), and in store design.

Citigroup and Prada's "Epicenter" store are two examples of brand experience design. The Citigroup case illustrates the complex strategic issues involved in implementing a brand experience for an entire corporation on a global scale. Prada's Epicenter shows the challenges of creating the right store design for the brand experience.

Citigroup: Shaping a Unified Brand Experience

In 2001, Citigroup, the world's largest financial company, which operates in more than 102 countries, launched a new brand identity organized around appeals to the customer experience. The company had merged in 1998 with Travelers Insurance, and a question on everybody's mind was how customers would regard the new colossus of financial and insurance services. The new identity involved bringing together many diverse businesses under the "Citi" name and a "Citi" logo and visuals.

With its new identity in place, the company began to reach out to convey that identity to customers. It set up new customer service stations in bank outlets and posted promises to customers right next to those stations. Designers revamped the Web site, the look and feel of the programs running on ATM machines, and created new direct-mail pieces.

The touchstone of a new brand advertising campaign in the United States was the experience of customers themselves. To promote and appeal to values other than the financial bottom line, Citigroup launched an all-text print and outdoor campaign focused on the experiential theme "Live richly."

Ads stated, "Be independently happy" and "It's a financial statement, not a scorecard" and "Collecting interest does not count as a hobby." Another ad suggested that it is more important to impress your children than your accountant.

Not everybody seemed happy with Citi's new ad campaign, however. On salon.com, writer Joseph Lamport derided the campaign as an "obscenity": "Are we . . . so morally and intellectually depleted," he asked, "that we will eagerly accept a pseudo-moral philosophy from a bank?" Lamport may have a point, but as always, the customer will be the ultimate arbiter.

In April 2002, the company continued in the vein of focusing on the customer by launching a new global print and TV advertising campaign shot in eight countries on five continents. "The advertising challenge was to communicate the multiple parts of the Citigroup story (a diverse product portfolio, global reach, deep roots, and stability) in a singular, powerful message," the press release stated.

Each ad emphasized one or more core strengths and concluded with a compelling fact and the definitive "This is Citigroup." The first execution, a 30-second commercial called "Umbrella," speaks to the global reach and diverse portfolio of products through vibrant visuals from around the world. Another ad depicts people from different lands, each with different needs, ranging from London's financial district ("some of us need to merge companies on different sides of the ocean") to a cabin in Vermont ("some of us need to buy groceries"). The ad campaign also related nicely to the company's core values, which focus on a diverse and caring work environment.

The brand experience theme appeared not only in advertising but also in the design and on the cover of the 2001 financial report. The company seems set to continue to redefine itself around the needs of its customers.

Prada's "Epicenter": Challenges of the In-Store Experience

Prada, the Italian high-end fashion brand firm, no longer believes in flagship stores; they believe in "epicenters." In 1999, the luxury retailer unveiled plans to construct four such epicenters: in New York, Los Angeles, San Francisco, and Tokyo. For the first, in New York's trendy SoHo district, Prada recruited the international guru architect Rem Koolhaas to design a "laboratory where the company can experiment with new forms of customer interaction." Constructed at a staggering cost of 40 million dollars, the 30,000 square-foot space occupies the former site of the Guggenheim Museum's SoHo branch. The store opened during the 2001 holiday season and was controversial from the start.

To understand why, we need to explain what an epicenter is, how the concept relates to the brand experience, and what Prada wanted to achieve with it. According to Koolhaas, expansion can represent a crisis for a brand: "In the typical case it spells the end of the brand as a creative enterprise and the beginning of the brand as a purely financial enterprise."[1] A manifestation of this danger is what Prada calls "the Flagship syndrome: a megalomaniac accumulation of the obvious that eliminates the last elements of surprise and mystery that cling to the brand, imprisoning it in a 'definitive' identity." The epicenter becomes for Prada a way to sidestep this danger. Rather than permanently freezing Prada's brand, the epicenter store "becomes a device that renews the brand by counteracting and stabilizing any received notion of what Prada is, does, or will become. The epicenter store functions as a conceptual window: a medium to broadcast future directions."

What does this all mean in practical terms? For Prada, the key words are *variety, exclusivity, changeability, service,* and *noncommercial.* Variety comes into play: stores should not be identical, and the same store can contain a variety of spaces.

FIGURE 5.1

New Prada store under construction in Tokyo. *Credit:* Photo by the author.

Exclusivity, a hallmark of any luxury brand, can also be expressed through the space, or how the store is perceived in a host city. Changeability—the perception of newness—is essential for keeping the brand vital and growing: the plan is that 60 percent of the business identity remains constant while 40 percent changes continually. As the brand grows, service is perceived as the key to maintaining the intimacy of a small company. Finally, Prada would like to use its space to foster ties with noncommercial, cultural enterprises: events such as fashion shows could be hosted in stores, and activities other than shopping could take place after store hours.

Prada set its sights very high with these concepts and tried to embody them in the epicenter store's look and feel.

The centerpiece of the SoHo store is a multistory curved wall (known as "the Wave") inlaid in zebra wood. On one side, the Wave features a bank of projections that can be used either as seating space for public events or as display space for shoes. Facing the Wave is a surface that can be tilted to create a stage or film projection space. Throughout the huge store, video monitors display arty images. Clothing is displayed in wire cages that glide around the floors. Changing rooms are equipped with glass walls that become opaque at the flip of a switch.

It looks and feels cool, but it doesn't work. When I first visited the epicenter soon after it was opened, I was overwhelmed by the architecture but disappointed by the store. The place was packed, not with customers but with architects and architecture students checking out the Wave and other physical features. The merchandise is crowded into the basement of the store and almost seems like an afterthought. As I walked out, I wondered how long it would take before the merchandising managers would scream *Enough! Enough!* and transform the space into an actual working store.

Prada and Koolhaas started out with intriguing and provocative ideas, but somewhere along the line the experiential platform for the brand got lost. As interesting as the concept of the epicenter space may be, it provides an inadequate brand experience. Customers end up being dwarfed by the large space, and Prada is left with a tourist attraction instead of a store. It is ironic that Prada's manifesto about "the Flagship syndrome" should have cautioned against megalomania, because in the end their store has turned out to be just that: more a work of Koolhaas megalomania than a functioning retail space.

How to Manage the Brand Experience

As discussed in Chapter 4, the experiential platform, consisting of an experiential positioning, an experiential value promise, and an overall implementation theme, includes viable knowledge about the desired customer experience. Moreover, the experiential platform has been developed to provide differentiation and value to customers. Therefore, the brand experience must follow straight from this platform.

As easy as this may sound, it is a tough management job. Many companies hire strategic consultants and branding experts to manage brand strategy. But these professionals often develop strategies without doing research or running preliminary tests. After the consulting work, management passes on the strategy to the implementers within and outside the firm: the design engineers, the packaging designers, the Web designers, the advertising agency, the store architects, and so on. These implementers often lack complete information about the strategy and thus pursue their own agendas (such as doing design and advertising that improves their chances of winning an award). Moreover, they rarely get together or have regular contact with one another. The piecemeal brand experience that results can leave customers cold, or worse, confused.

To ensure business success, CEM must be a seamless process that starts with customer insight, continues with a platform that includes customer input, and ends in a customer-experience-driven implementation.

A CEM project works only if all the implementers have a detailed understanding of the experiential platform. Such an understanding will facilitate their task tremendously and ensure that the early analysis and strategy work are not lost in the implementation. Moreover, *everybody* on the project needs to be customer-oriented: the in-house engineers and designers, the external design houses, and the outsourced communication providers.

The Three Key Aspects of the Brand Experience

In the following sections, we zoom in on three key aspects of the brand experience: the *product experience,* the *look and feel,* and *experiential communications* (see Figure 5.2). I introduce a few pertinent concepts that are helpful in managing these aspects of the brand experience.

FIGURE 5.2
The Three Key Aspects of the Brand Experience

125

The Product Experience

The product is the focal point of the customer experience. The experience, of course, includes the functional attributes of the product—how well the thing works. But with the high-quality products generally available now, such functional features are hardly worth consideration. Consumers take for granted that their computers or refrigerators or cars will do what they are supposed to do. For consumers today, other product features are more important. These *experiential features* serve as a springboard for a customer's brand experience.

For example, the ingredients ginger, gingko biloba, and echinacea in Jamba Juice fruit juices or their packaged equivalents, Odwalla, Fresh Samantha, and Naked, aren't just there for their ostensible health benefits. They are there because they are cool, Eastern-inspired, and holistically natural, and thus create an interesting and engaging experience for consumers.

Another example is the infrared port in your personal digital assistant (PDA). Very few people seem to use this feature or even know how to use it. It has certainly fallen short of replacing actual business cards, as it was forecast to do. (In the early years of the PalmPilot, the company ran a print ad showing a group of businesspeople around a conference table, happily "beaming" virtual cards to each other.) However, the infrared feature remains an attractive experiential feature because it catches your attention, whether you use it or not, and it provides the opportunity to connect with colleagues in a new way.

Experiential features are also important in B2B markets. Some new procedures, techniques, and operations in many factories offer few functional advances. However, they provide a great high-tech experience for the technology and operations departments.

There is much more to the experience a product provides than its functional and experiential features. An important consideration is *how* a product works.

Every product designer, programmer, or mechanical engineer will tell you that there are different ways to solve any given problem. For these experts, solutions, at a gut level, fall into two categories: elegant and nonelegant. Moreover, engineers are not the only ones who think in these experiential terms. Customers notice, too. They may not be able to look into the machine or see a blueprint of it. But they will notice by interacting with the product whether its underlying designs or programs are elegant. An elegant solution works with grace. The grace may consist in its simplicity, uniqueness, or intricacy. No matter what it is, the product with this magic is seen as superior.

Finally, there is the aesthetic appeal of the product. In 1997, I coauthored a book called *Marketing Aesthetics*[2] that focused on the customer's sensory experience with a product and communications. Indeed, the product's aesthetics—its design, its colors and shapes, and so on—should not be considered separately from the functional and experiential features of the product and how it works. By considering the experience in entirety, all the product's aspects should come together to make it a "pearl of engineering." It is *beautiful*; it has a chance to end up in the design collection of the Museum of Modern Art, and even if it does not, it will have its own community of loyal fans.

Engineers and product designers need to incorporate experience into product development, so that the product provides experiential value as well as functional value to customers. Only then does the product deliver on the experiential value promise, or EVP, that makes up a key part of the experiential platform. The Apple i-Mac is a product line that delivers on the EVP. Since their launch in the late 1990s, Apple has cranked out one instant classic after another. These machines work (not something necessarily to be taken for granted, as many a Mac user of the mid-1990s can tell you). But it's not just that. It is how they work and their aesthetics: the screen that can be rotated to almost any angle, the pulsating light when the computer goes to sleep, the candy-store beauty of the Mac OSX operating system. What is more, such successful product experiences consistently relate to Apple's experiential platform of standing out in design, being user-friendly, and being creative. Chapter 7 discusses Apple's continuous innovation in detail.

The Look and Feel

The look and feel surrounding the product (also referred to as "brand identity") is another key aspect of the brand experience. Customers do not get just the product features. They get a product with a name, logo, and signage on a bottle or container or packaging, and they buy it in a store or on the Internet, where it is displayed in a certain way. The look and feel thus includes the visual identity (name, logo, signage), packaging, the store design and merchandising, and the graphic design elements on a Web site.

Some experts seem to believe that there is not much that one can say or show in a name, logo, or signage; so they are satisfied with boring, uninformative, and abstract names and designs that can be difficult to remember. They argue that packaging leaves little space for extended imagery and messages and certainly not for spelling out the full-fledged experiential platform.

Not true! In fact, there is a trend toward more detailed and informative product packaging, but with an experiential twist in the imagery and messages that appear as part of a brand identity. In the new fruit juice market that I referred to earlier, the experiential positioning and EVP appear right on the plastic bottle.

For example, in addition to the routine nutrition facts required by the FDA, the bottle of "Naked Food" Juice includes experiential photography and a cool product statement (the product sitting in front of me now, "Protein Zone," has the tagline "Because you can't drink a steak"). It also makes a strong attempt to communicate the experiential platform:

Naked Food-Juice was first squeezed in 1983 in Santa Monica Beach, CA (Fresh Fruit Capital of the World). Everyday since we have bottled the freshest, most delicious juices, with this simple mission in mind: To every man, woman & child moving 100 MPH in this crazy, 10-lane highway-world, with no off-ramp for nourishment, Naked Food-Juice delivers your daily dose of vitamins, energy & yum. These are the bare essentials to satisfy your body, psyche & soul. If you eat or drink nothing else . . . get Naked.

Does it work? Consider Odwalla. In 1980, three musicians founded Odwalla Juice Company in a backyard in Santa Cruz,

California. They wanted to raise cash to "create musical and multimedia presentations for local schools and cultural events to educate people on cultural diversity and the environment." Odwalla received national attention in May 2000 when it merged with Fresh Samantha and became the leading natural juice company in the United States with over 5,000 retail locations. By 2001, Odwalla was generating revenues of $123 million, and in March 2002, the Coca-Cola Company bought Odwalla Juice Company for $182 million.

These fruit juices deliver their platform in the brand experience in a humorous, cool way that is totally unlike the stodgy look and feel of the cereal boxes just across the aisle in the supermarket. But wait. Nowadays, even the back of my good old Cheerios box has imagery (a heart, two children hugging each other, a father and his son). And the text ("the Nurturing Corner: Here are Five Great Ways to Show Your Kids You Care") relates cleverly and creatively to the product's positioning of being "heart-healthy." Thus, the experiential approach is becoming a broad-based trend in consumer goods, despite what the experts thought.

But what about products we receive as businesspeople? We still don't see similar design messages on most packaging of B2B products. The B2B markets present a tremendous untouched opportunity for relevant differentiation and added value by treating packaging as more than just a way of protecting and identifying what is inside. For example, why isn't there useful information on the packaging of my printer cartridge about how printing and sharing documents can help me organize my work more efficiently?

Don't be afraid to reveal your positioning in the look and feel. Your positioning of the company and its brands is not a secret that you need to protect from theft by your competitors. If you are trying to hide your position from your competitors, you are likely hiding it from your customers, too! Once you have developed an experiential positioning, make sure to communicate it as much as possible in the look and feel. If you are worried about your competitors, there are ways to protect the look and feel once it is in the public domain; we will get to them in a moment.

Always remember: an experiential platform is unlike the traditional positioning statement that is buried in a thick strategic consulting report but never comes to life. The platform provides tangible guidance for implementation in everything that you put in front of the customer.

Experiential Communications

One of the holy concepts of traditional advertising and communications has been the unique selling proposition (USP). It is product-centered and outcome-focused because features and benefits are all that matter to the traditional marketer. It is sales driven because advertisers need to prove that their ads sell.

Yet, there is more to a product than its features and benefits and outcome functionality. Even though the objective must be increased sales (from new customers, current customers, and add-on selling), it is unlikely that propositioning the customer in such a way will do the trick. Today's products often lack functional differentiation. Today's consumers, especially young customers, are market-savvy and hate being manipulated.

Box 5.1

Right on Target

Checked out a Target store lately? In case you haven't noticed, the Minneapolis-based discount store chain has been making some radical changes to its brand. Target was founded in 1961, the same year that two other American discount chains, Wal-Mart and Kmart, were first opened. Now Target is out to prove that all discount stores are not the same.

So what *can* you get at Target? How about a housewares line designed by world-renowned architect Michael Graves? Or a bed and bath line by avant-garde designer Todd Oldham, star of MTV's *House of Style*. Or housewares by Philippe Starck? Hardly discount-store fare. The idea is to use good design as a differentiating factor and to make good design relatively inexpensive. While Wal-Mart stands for low price and low price only, Target promotes fashion and lifestyle as well as "fast, fun, and friendly" service in the store. Not a bad strategy given the success of the VW Beetle and the revised Apple computer in the late 1990s.

To increase the volume of shoppers in its stores, Target has expanded into the grocery business. Once again, it differentiates its brand from Wal-Mart by adding higher-ticket products to the shopping basket. You can buy, for example, a Fuji apple that has been screened for sweetness with infrared equipment to measure its sugar level, and temperature-tested bananas that do not ripen too fast.

Target is obsessed with measuring and monitoring the experience. Managers keep thick report cards for every store. At the end of most aisles is a red service phone for Target customers (called "guests" in company lingo) and

---

Box 5.1 Continued

headquarters gets a printout of how many times the phone went on and how fast it was picked up. "The challenge is getting all 1,100 stores to run the same way and deliver that Target experience every day," says Bart Butzer, executive vice president of Target Stores.*

Awareness and management of the customer experience has permeated Target's redesign of its brand. The company is performing very well, with $39.9 billion becoming the second largest retailer after Wal-Mart. Analysts are impressed with earnings and revenues and with a higher profit margin. Target is becoming more efficient than its main rival, Wal-Mart.

---

*Constance L. Hays, "Can Target Thrive in Wal-Mart's Cross Hairs?" *New York Times* (June 9, 2002), sec. 3, p. 1.

Therefore, advertising has to provide value; it must inform and entertain. Otherwise, the customer will not allow the message through.

Advertisers and other communication providers should thus replace the USP with an ESP, an *experiential selling paradigm*. The ESP is not a soft-sell version of the USP; it is an entirely new way of thinking—a new paradigm—that explains how advertising can be used to implement the brand experience. The ESP grows out of the experiential platform and its three components: the experiential positioning, the experiential value promise (EVP), and the overall implementation theme. The experiential positioning is useful for designing the overall tone of the ad. (Should the execution be aggressive or soft? Should it appeal to the intellect or emotions?) The EVP is helpful in specifying what the ad sells in an experiential sense. (What does the customer get from the product through the product look and feel, through the community that purchases the product?) Finally, the overall implementation theme is relevant for the creative effort and for laying out advertising's role among other experience providers. (Should advertising and its media assume a central or supporting role? What media plan would be most effective in our advertising and ensure that other experience providers are effective as well?)

What do communications that follow this new paradigm look like? Typically, they provide the brand with a noteworthy, experiential personality showing the customer's experience when using the product. Coca-Cola's 2002 outdoor ad campaign for lemon-flavored Diet Coke shows a close-up of the delighted face of a person who has presumably just consumed the product. In an integrated ad and web campaign targeting professional cinematographers, Kodak's motion picture imaging division asked established filmmakers, who shot movies on Kodak film, to share their professional philosophy and describe their experience in using Kodak film. Such campaigns can develop a strong cult following, as Dell's "Dude" campaign has shown.

Experiential communications that follow the paradigm also provide relevant context for the customer. A successful B2B ad campaign that focused on business leaders and decision makers featured contexts calling for an IBM solution. In one ad, executives are called for an emergency meeting because the server and

Web site are down interrupting all customer contact: "That's when it hits you. You are so ready for IBM."

Finally, a specific form of communication (e.g., the ad campaign) is usually integrated with other communications. As part of its Life Savers personality campaign discussed in Chapter 4, Kraft spent $15 million in print and outdoor consumer promotion and on the Internet from February through September 2002. The print ads were placed in special themed personality magazines such as *Sports Illustrated*'s swimsuit issue, *People Magazine*'s Oscar issue and its 60 Most Beautiful People issue. As part of a consumer promotions campaign, consumers could win a prize when they found Life Savers with a "winning personality"—a filled-in hole with embossed candy. Finally, the Web site, candystand.com, featured new personalities, and consumers could find out what their favorite Life Saver personality revealed about them. We will take a closer look at the power of integration in Chapter 8.

Protecting the Brand Experience

A CEM initiative is a major undertaking, and companies are reasonably concerned about protecting what they have developed. Different elements of the project have varying degrees of vulnerability. The brand experience is the implementation domain that competitors can copy most easily. In contrast, the customer interface is dynamic and thus is much more difficult to copy, especially if it involves customized face-to-face interactions with customers or an interactive experience on the Internet or via mobile devices. Continuous innovation is also difficult to copy (excluding corporate espionage). New product development and marketing innovation within the company is open to public inspection only when it is launched. At that point, the new product may be patent-protected, or the new marketing events will include lots of creative and dynamic elements and therefore be hard to imitate.

Because the brand experience, being static and public, is easier to copy, a company may decide to protect it legally. Product design is subject to patent protection. The look and feel, and messages of certain experiential communications can be protected as part of intellectual property law (via registered trademarks and service marks). Even the brand experience in an entire store can be protected if it presents a unique brand dress and experience.

In 1999, Sephora, the chain of cosmetics retail stores owned by LVMH, sued Federated Department Stores' Macy's Division for trade dress infringements. The lawsuit claimed that Federated had copied the original and distinctive look and feel of Sephora in its "Souson" branded stores in the San Francisco Bay area, in Southern California, and in the Union Square Macy's store in San Francisco. Sephora argued that such copying would result in highly similar customer experiences and confusion. Sephora had first opened its doors in 1996 in Paris and by 2000 had more than 200 stores worldwide (including more than 50 in the United States).

I served as an expert witness for Sephora. I rarely serve as a legal expert, but the case was such a blatant example of copying that I decided to accept this invitation. Indeed, when I visited the stores, I noticed a striking similarity in all the core design elements and in the resulting brand experience:

- As in the Sephora stores, the Souson stores had a spacious and contemporary layout and design. Display shelves were located along the walls and horizontally to the storefront. The open register areas were in the center of the stores. The stores had two entrance areas to the left and to the right of the storefront.

- As in Sephora stores, the color scheme of the Souson floors had a black and white "marble stone" look. Ceiling spotlights provided dramatic lighting; cylindrical light strips that were part of the product shelves and directed toward the products also provided lighting.

- As in Sephora stores, Souson used music to create an atmosphere. The music, including contemporary pop or jazz, made a statement about the store atmosphere.

- As in Sephora stores, fragrance designer brands in the Souson stores were displayed in alphabetical order, and the names of the major brands were featured on top of the display shelves.

- Both Sephora and Souson salespeople wore contemporary, black uniforms. Shopping baskets were available for the customer next to or near the register area.

- Like Sephora, Souson carried its own store brand of lipstick. Like the corresponding Sephora product, the Souson lipsticks were labeled with three-digit numbers and a letter that referred to the look and style of the lipstick. The lipstick products were encased in a tube in such a way that parts of the product could be seen through the tube.

What mattered in my opinion was not whether all the individual elements of the stores were identical (and, surprisingly many were); the critical consideration was whether these elements, as a whole, could induce a certain customer experience and confuse customers.

Indeed, the judge who granted Sephora's request for a preliminary injunction against Federated ruled that store visitors might be confused into thinking that they had entered a Sephora-owned or a Sephora-operated facility. The two companies settled the case in 2000. Terms of the settlement were not disclosed.

Rarely is a case that clear-cut. More likely, imitation will be ambiguous and thus not subject to legal procedures. A company should therefore consider using other business procedures to protect the brand experience; for example, requiring confidentiality agreements or not disclosing the suppliers of design elements. Also, there is an old rule in business: the first brand enjoys a "first mover advantage." This advantage also applies in managing the brand experience. Customers appreciate when a company is first; such companies quickly gain customer loyalty and often become a classic. Being first can be newsworthy, and once other firms imitate your company, you can get the word out that imitation is the highest form of flattery.

"Brand Stripping and Dressing": A Method for Managing the Brand Experience

Brand stripping and dressing is a management and research methodology for developing, planning, and coordinating a brand experience. This experience must follow directly from and include all the relevant aspects of the experiential platform.

For an existing brand, this often requires stripping the brand, in several steps, down to its bare essentials to eliminate all nonessential and undesirable designs and executions of the brand experience (packaging, advertising, Web design, etc.). Next, the brand is dressed up again to enrich the brand experience with new designs and executions.

The procedure can be done internally and in conjunction with implementation experts (internal design team, ad agency, Web designers). I recommend seeking customer input as well. The ideal procedure usually has two steps, starting with an expert brand stripping and dressing and following up with customer input (e.g., focus groups, individual interviews, or other research techniques).

I have used this methodology many times in executive training and consulting engagements with companies. The insights gained from this methodology can be extraordinary. The outcome usually includes quantitative ratings and qualitative insights as well as creative ideas from experts and customers. Quantitative information (e.g., about the importance and sequencing of design and communication elements) can be derived from the order in which design elements or communications are stripped off and added. Qualitative insights result from an analysis of the discussions that occur before removing or adding a design or communication element. The creative insights are gained in the dressing sequence as participants suggest new design or communication elements and new overall design or communication solutions.

The last part of the procedure is a qualitative and quantitative assessment of the degree of duplicated design elements in various executions (e.g., in the ads, packaging, on the Web site) as well as the overall degree of consistency and experience resulting from each execution. This check assures that all aspects of the brand experience are properly aligned and result in the desired experience.

Conclusion

In this chapter, we discussed concepts and a methodology for managing the first of three implementation domains: the brand experience. The most important task is to make sure that the brand experience follows from the experiential platform, in particular, the overall implementation theme. Once you have decided on this theme, you can move on to the specific aspects of designing the brand experience (the product, the look and feel surrounding it, and experiential communications). In some situations, you may need to protect the brand experience legally to prevent other firms from copying your identity and trade dress.

The focus throughout was on the predesigned, static implementation domain. Chapter 6 deals with the dynamic customer interface that may take place face-to-face in a store, in a sales call, through a call center, online, or via mobile communications.

Structuring the Customer Interface

The customer interface is the second key implementation domain of the experiential platform. This interface refers to the dynamic exchange of information and service that occurs between the customer and a company—in person, over the phone, online, or in any other way. An interactive exchange occurs when a depositor uses an ATM at a bank, when a businessperson checks in at a hotel desk, when a customer returns an item in a store, or when people engage in a chat session on the Internet.

The customer interface can enhance—or degrade—the customer experience that has been built through the brand experience. Therefore, it is necessary to structure the customer interface carefully. It must follow the overall implementation theme of the experiential platform, and its content and form must be based on customer input.

The CEM approach to the customer interface goes far beyond the customer relationship management (CRM) software and database management technologies developed in recent years. Most CRM solutions merely record what can easily be tracked: the history and transactions of customer-company contacts. The solutions address only certain interface touchpoints (e.g., call centers, e-mail exchanges, purchase transactions). The standardized CRM software packages are difficult to customize and do not capture any of the nonverbal information that is so critical to the customer experience. Finally, they are expensive to implement ($40 to $60 million for a mid- to large-size firm) and provide little customer-relevant differentiation. To provide a truly satisfying experience for their customers, companies need to go beyond what CRM offers.

Designing and managing the customer interface can be a complex task, beginning with an understanding of the interface itself. For most companies, the customer interface includes three types of exchanges and interactions:

1. *Face-to-face.* The face-to-face interface includes exchanges and interactions that occur in a store (for end consumers) or through the company's field sales force or service personnel (for B2B customers). Some offerings such as consulting services, counseling, and entertainment are delivered to the customer entirely face-to-face.

2. *Personal-but-distant.* Personal-but-distant exchanges and interactions occur via phone or fax, or in writing. Like the face-to-face interface, this interface is tailored to the

individual customer, the difference being that the customer and the company representative are not in the same physical space.

3. *Electronic.* The electronic interface includes exchanges and interactions on an e-commerce site, via e-mail or a short messages system (SMS). This kind of interface may appear to be personal, but it often follows a template and is the product of mass-produced communications.

The following two cases show how an interface can be structured around the customer experience. NikePark is a dynamic and exciting environmental and online interface for today's youth. Next, the interface project launched at Hilton Hotels in 2002 is a guest-focused program that goes far beyond many customer relationship management projects.

NikePark: A Dynamic Interface for a Performance-Driven Brand

With a global event timed to coincide with the 2002 Fifa World Cup in Korea and Japan, Nike demonstrated what a cutting-edge, dynamic interface for a performance-driven sports brand can be like. At "NikeParks" around the world, people could walk in, sign up, and join teams to compete in a series of intense and fast-paced games. In a sense, Nike staged its own amateur, walk-in World Cup for fans all over the world.

NikeParks were set up in cities around the world—Tokyo, Seoul, Mexico City, London, Beijing, Los Angeles, São Paulo, Berlin, Paris, Buenos Aires, Madrid, Rotterdam, and Rome, among others. The scope of the event varied from city to city.

FIGURE 6.1
Outside NikePark in Tokyo. *Credit:* Photo by the author.

In big soccer markets, like the World Cup host cities Seoul and Tokyo, Nike took over an entire professional sports stadium for four full weeks; in smaller markets like Los Angeles (the only U.S. venue), Nike set up one-day NikeParks in neighborhood parks.

Whatever the venue, the game was the same. Teams of three people, who could sign up together or individually, competed in three-minute special soccer skills games such as Foot Volley, Funnel, and Speed Shot—known as Scorpion K.O. games. Winners went on to the next round; losers went home. The big winners competed for the opportunity to go to the finals in Buenos Aires.

FIGURE 6.2
Soccer ball display at NikePark Tokyo. *Credit:* Photo by the author.

I visited the Tokyo NikePark in June 2002. Nike had chosen as its venue Yoyogi Stadium, situated near the Harajuku area, which is popular with young people. The entire area was transformed into a multimedia world devoted to soccer. As the slogan said, "I'm not going there to meet the pros. I'm going there to play football." The entire experience was built around playing the game. Outside the stadium, playing courts were set up where small teams could compete. Inside there were more such courts, in addition to practice areas, a table-football area, a penalty shot area where players and goalies could face off, and the special three-person games that made up the tournament. One training area featured video screens with major players executing special moves; in this unique environment, participants could practice moves while watching their heroes on the video screen. NTT DoCoMo, the innovative Japanese communications company, had set up a booth where visitors could be photographed playing soccer and instantly send the photos to friends as SMS files.

Through the NikeParks and the worldwide Scorpion K.O. tournament, Nike provided a way for soccer fans to experience the excitement of the World Cup in an active—and interactive—experiential way. In the NikePark, the customers were the stars. The atmosphere was dark and dramatic, more like a disco than a sports stadium, especially at night. Video displays were everywhere, set off by lighting in strong primary colors. The brand experience was targeted and sophisticated, not in your face with names and logos. There was a retailing area for Nike shoes and sports merchandise, but the NikeParks did not focus on commercialism. Nike built them to celebrate soccer playing and in the process created a unique customer interface.

Nike's soccer Web site, www.nikefootball.com (www.nikesoccer.com in the United States), provided visitors with information about the NikeParks—locations, dates, visiting soccer celebrities, and so on. What is more, the Web site experience was carefully customized for local markets. A special message appeared on the site after the NikePark closed at each venue. For the London venue, visitors got this cool message: "NikePark SKO has now finished. But you don't have to. Play on." For the Mexico City venue, readers got a message tailored to Mexico's very courteous communication style: "*El torneo ha finalizado. Gracias a todas las personas que hicieron suyo el NikePark.* [The tournament has finished. Thanks to all those people who made NikePark their own.]" The Singapore venue held a hint of technological mystery: "secret locations revealed only to registered participants via SMS." At the conclusion of each local installment of the tournament, results and photos of the winners were posted on the site.

But the Web site is far more than an online brochure for live events; it provides an array of rich and engaging experiences for visitors. Click on the "tournament" button and you are drawn into a bizarre and mesmerizing story about a "Secret Tournament" among eight fictitious teams, held aboard a grimy oil tanker moored at night in unspecified waters. Visitors "enter" the tanker and find a small soccer pitch in the rusting and riveted interior, lit only by bare bulbs. The site's navigation bars are done in rough, stenciled lettering such as you might see on cargo crates; rollover menus are in similarly rough lettering and move ever so slightly to the motion of the ship. Buttons are rusty "iron" panels that roll down on chains. Sound effects suggest the pulsing of the tanker's engines.

The amount of content on the site is staggering. Information about the eight colorful teams—including the Funk Seoul Brothers, Toros Locos, and Tutto Bene—is available, and extensive video files—both live and animated, and beautifully done—document the tournament from quarter-finals through the final and on to the rematch. Visitors can watch "favorite moments" from the tournament and can choose to view them in slow motion or even frame-by-frame to get a real appreciation of the virtuosity of the moves.

A soccer fan could happily spend hours on this site, and not just watching. A series of Scorpion K.O. games are available for visitors to play online. Each player gets a team of three, and

FIGURE 6.3

SCHMITT Shoe created on Nike.com. *Credit:* Courtesy of SCHMITT.

sophisticated technology allows you to "train" your team members in a particular skill before you jump into tournament play. Visitors pit their teams against a computer-controlled team and vie for prizes like an autographed Geo Chrome Ball, Secret Tournament T-shirt, and the grand prize—the Ultimate Nike soccer gear pack.

To complete the interface experience, visitors can buy Nike products on the site. Buyers can customize their shoes (see Figure 6.3), selecting the style, the kind of tread they want, and their preferred color combinations. They can even request a monogram of their name and jersey number if they like.

Hilton: Improving Communication and Guest Focus to Enhance the Service Experience

In 2002, Hilton launched on an ambitious interface project to improve communication and services with its customers.

The new program was targeted toward Hilton's highest-value customers and business accounts, as well as new high-worth customers. It was led by Rebecca Wyatt, Vice President of Brand Integration, and Bala Subramanian, Senior Vice President for Customer and Brand Strategies. The goal of the project was to increase loyalty, therefore impacting "share of wallet," as share in a particular category is often called.

Cross-selling across the various Hilton brands (Hilton, Embassy Suites, Doubletree, Hampton Inns, Hilton Garden Inn, Homewood Suites, and the international Conrad line) was of particular importance in the new project. The initiative built on an earlier brand architecture project, of which I had been a part. The objective of that effort had been to set up the brand in such a way that it would create the image of one company while keeping some distinct identities and facilitating cross-selling.

The Hilton project team first identified 17 critical touchpoints that could enrich the customer experience, or for which, in case of a failure, there would be recovery programs. These touchpoints—which identified related elements—were reservations (via the phone, the Web, or an intermediary); brand communications; sales and account management's communications; arrival and check-in (including first impressions of the guest room); wake-up and messaging; in-room entertainment; Hilton HHonors marketing and communications, tracking, and enrollment; guest assistance; room service; concierge; and business service center. The goal was to reengineer these critical touchpoints to deliver the right customer experience, ideally in a customized way based on prior preferences, needs, and importance.

149

For example, customers who have stayed numerous times in a Doubletree hotel may not need or want an elaborate check-in that includes one of the managers walking them to their room and explaining facilities. These customers may view this check-in not as personal service but as a waste of time. However, a new customer, or the Doubletree customer arriving at a Conrad hotel for the first time, might highly value such personal attention. Thus, the system would need to select specific service features based on the customer's prior experience and preferences.

To design a successful customer interface at these critical touchpoints, the team had to find appropriate answers for six specific groups of questions:

1. What is the real "moment of truth"? What are the customer's needs, expectations, and wants at this particular touchpoint? How does this vary by customer segment?

2. What is the ideal service interaction? What are the service delivery imperatives? How do we deliver great anticipatory service?

3. How do we personalize the service interaction and use the critical touchpoint to foster relationship building? How does this vary by customer segment?

4. How do we use the critical touchpoint and the interaction to bring each brand's values to life? How do we make the brand more distinct and much more relevant to targeted customer and travel occasion segments?

5. How do we create differentiated service signals that can be owned by the brand? How do we create barriers to switching?

6. What knowledge, analytics, and technology are required to make all this happen?

Let's look at how Hilton is implementing its new approach by 2003. We will take a look at one personal-but-distant touchpoint: the reservation. Here is a script that Hilton developed for telephone reservations. The model customer is Ms. Janet Jones, CFO of a major entertainment company, Hilton HHonors member since 1997:

- Thank you for calling Hilton HHonors Preferred Member Services. How can we be of assistance today, Ms. Jones?

  Answers within two rings. Calls by name (phone number recognition where possible).

- You're traveling to Alpharetta, 2 nights, starting August 22. I'll check your preferred hotel at that location: the Hilton Garden Inn Northpoint.

  We greatly appreciate your extensive travel with the Hilton Family of Brands. While I'm checking availability for the Hilton Garden Inn . . . I see that you stayed at our Hilton Fisherman's Wharf last night. Did you enjoy your stay?

  Unfortunately, there is no availability that night at the Hilton Garden Inn. However, I can confirm you for the Embassy Suites, Alpharetta . . . a short 2 blocks away. I see that you stay at our Embassy Suites Hotels often as well.

  Shall I reserve you a room on the second floor . . . a king bed . . . with feather pillows. Is this correct?

  Confirms availability, member data, and preferences.

- Per your personal preferences, we will immediately send you an e-mail confirmation that includes the hotel address and map. Let me verify your e-mail address. May I make any other reservations or assist you in any other way today?

Books room. Verifies profile information. Offers further assistance.

The script reflects the way Hilton's technology enables the reservations agent to see Ms. Jones's transaction record with Hilton and her preferences for room location and various amenities. In this way, Hilton can provide a personalized customer interface for each of its returning visitors.

The campaign extends beyond the telephone interface to include personalized e-mail confirmations and reminders, as well as personal greetings at check-in and in the room. After ending her stay, Ms. Jones will receive a thank-you and follow-up e-mail from the hotel. The e-mail asks her if there is anything that Hilton could have done to improve her experience, and confirms her HHonors points posted and her account balance. Hilton's program ensures that every aspect of the customer's experience will be memorable and pleasing.

What about the program from an organizational point of view? What does Hilton hope to gain through this program, beyond happy customers? The quantitative objectives linked to Hilton's program were ambitious:

- To increase customer satisfaction (defined as top box ratings) to 75 percent.
- To increase share-of-wallet of top-tier customers and key accounts from 40 percent to 45 percent.
- To increase retention of first-time, at-trial users by 10 percent.

- To increase cross-brand stays by 5 percent.
- To increase the percentage of Internet-enabled bookings to 30 percent.
- To reduce the cost of Internet-enabled bookings from $6.00 to $3.00.

Hilton completed Phase I of its launch of this program in April 2002. Additional aspects of the program will be implemented in quarterly releases. Early indicators of success include an increase in customer perception of being "Recognized as a VIP" and "recognized as a returning guest." Cross-sell revenues are up by over 25 percent. Internet-enabled booking costs are expected to be below $4.00 in 2003 and Internet reservations are expected to exceed 16 percent in 2003, and 30 percent by 2007. Since Phase I was enabled in April 2002 through the end of August, 10.2 million guests have stayed with the Hilton Family of Hotels, of which 3.3 million were identified as "Best Guests." Over 400,000 guests would not have been recognized as HHonors members at the appropriate tier without the newly enabled back-end matching functionality.

Moreover, the number of calls to the HHonors Service Center due to points and miles not being awarded for stays are down by approximately 30 percent, and calls to update profiles are down by over 45 percent.

Its focus on the customer experience and measurement of its impact goes beyond many customer relationship programs. Thus, it can serve as a blueprint for incorporating customer experience into a service and loyalty program at every touchpoint.

The CEM Approach to the Customer Interface

A hotel visit, a store visit, a salesperson's visit in the customer's office or home, a follow-up call, a visit to the company Web site—all these exchanges and interactions offer opportunities to connect with customers, delight them, provide them with the right information efficiently, and enrich their lives. Moreover, a company can differentiate itself and its products by designing the right interactive store environment, by hiring and training the right people, and by setting up the right Web site, exchanges, and interactions at the various customer connection points.

As part of a CEM project, the company must collect customer input when designing and structuring the interface. In designing the customer interface, the foremost questions are behavioral: What does a customer want to do in a store? How does the customer want to follow up? What does the customer want to do on a Web site?

The company also must link the customer interface to the experiential platform that it created based on an understanding of the customer's experiential world. In addition, the customer interface must be integrated with the two other pillars of implementation: the brand experience and continuous innovation. This means that the dynamic exchanges and interactions that occur as part of the interface must enhance and reinforce the product image, its look and feel, and all brand communications. Moreover, looking forward, the company's plans for innovation should include new approaches to the customer interface.

How can a company achieve all that? In Chapter 4, we discussed how the experiential platform culminates in an overall

154

implementation theme (e.g., "energy in a bottle" for Red Bull). This theme must be clear and distinctive and be focused on customer experience to ensure that the interface is strategically focused and integrated with all other aspects of the implementation.

In 1999 and 2001, I had the pleasure of working with the leading organizer of management programs in Latin America, the HSM Group. The HSM Group organizes training workshops, conferences, and other training programs at major convention centers, in small hotel rooms, and online for executives all over Latin America. Its customers are not only the consumers of these learning products, but also B2B customers such as speakers and consultants, like myself who work with the HSM Group on delivering content, and the human resources personnel within organizations who decide which of HSM's products to offer employees. In all its interfaces with all its customers, HSM focuses on the same goal, based on the overall implementation theme of providing "outstanding, personalized service and easy and accessible learning." The company conveys this theme in everything it does, from hiring the best personnel, to training them in service and customer interactions, and testing its online communications over and over again before they go live.

Three Key Issues in Interface Design

To structure the customer interface and integrate its touchpoints (i.e., a store, phone calls with customers, a Web site) the company must address three key issues: the right mix of essence and flexibility; the right mix of style and substance; and time in relationship to the interface (see Figure 6.4).

Essence and Flexibility

The right interface has the appropriate mix of essence and flexibility. To structure a customer interface, it is necessary to figure out its essence (e.g., key operations, interactions, and exchanges). How is the customer supposed to be greeted? What is supposed to happen during the contact? How should we follow-up? On the other hand, flexibility is also essential. Flexibility turns a sales space into a living space. Flexibility allows customers to perceive service staff not as robots but as humans. And flexibility is necessary so that the interface appears fresh and up-to-date.

Washington Mutual, a Seattle-based bank, is changing the customer banking experience by getting rid of the teller

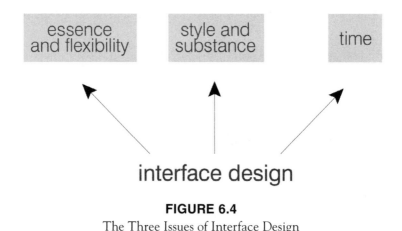

FIGURE 6.4
The Three Issues of Interface Design

156

barricaded behind a counter with thick Plexiglas. In a concept the company calls "Occasio" (Latin for "favorable opportunity"), Washington Mutual has designed new-style branches that look and feel more like retail stores than traditional bank settings. Entering an Occasio branch, the customer is first greeted by a "concierge" who escorts them to the appropriate area. For customers with children, a kids' play area is available to keep them entertained. There are no desks to be found in the branch. Instead, bank representatives work at electronic "teller towers." Others roam the floor helping customers with hand-held "e-tellers." Staff are dressed casually in khakis rather than formal banking attire. What a concept! And it is a true breakthrough in the realm of customer interface.

Style and Substance

The right interface is also about the right mix of style and substance. Style, in this context, refers to the manner of expressing the essence and flexibility of the interface. Substance refers to tangibles associated with it. Often an interface is unbalanced: too much style (lots of opening hype, fake friendliness), too little sales substance. On the other hand, a lot of the cold calls that companies make to customers are all about substance (getting you to make a purchase) without any charm or style. Web sites that err on the style side often present too much fancy animation that ends up getting in the customer's way; the ones that err on the side of substance present pages and pages of text that are hard to plow through. Whether it is a store, a phone call, or a Web site, a delightful customer experience requires a balanced mix of style and substance.

Time

Interface exchanges and interactions, by their very nature, extend over time. This raises the issue of how the customer contact should be phased over time. How should contact be initiated to make the experience delightful? How long should the contact last? What should be the key transition points? When is it desirable for the customer to leave, and how can we get him or her to return?

The three issues that I discussed are relevant for every type of customer interface—whether it is a store, a sales visit, or an Internet site.

Customer research should determine the structuring of a given interface along these three dimensions. "Natural habitat research," a technique discussed in Chapter 3, can be useful for gaining insights about a desirable store interface. Role-playing a sales encounter can provide guidance for structuring a sales call. Observing how customers browse Web sites when searching for a given product category or when they have a specific online goal is worthwhile for gaining insights about how to structure the home page of a Web site, with its icons and links, and its browsing and navigation systems.

Interconnecting Interface Touchpoints

Relating face-to-face, personal-but-distant, and electronic touchpoints to one another is a management challenge that many companies are facing since the advent of the Internet into a selling and service interface. Now, service and commerce occurs not only through face-to-face or personal-but-distant communication (such as over the phone) but in a standardized electronic format. Many companies are not even trying to relate these different interfaces; others have done it successfully.

Consider the luxury goods market. Luxury goods companies understood the power of the personal customer interface long before most other companies gave it much thought. They have to. Their products are expensive and their customers affluent enough to purchase nearly anything they please. Luxury products tend to be of universally high quality, so product features and benefits are far less important in the decision process than the customer's overall experience.

As a result, luxury retailers do everything they can to ensure that customers have a pleasant and satisfying in-store experience: beautiful store design, a sophisticated ambience, salespeople who ensure that customers find exactly what they need and have it delivered exactly when they need it.

With the advent of e-commerce, luxury companies faced the daunting task of translating the luxury experience online. In fact, some luxury companies are still holding back, unsure that the Internet can ever provide the kind of experience their customers expect. One pioneer company, however, made an early entry into the world of e-commerce, and they got it right the first time: Steuben.com.

A subsidiary of Corning, Steuben produces glass designs—vases, sculptures, and decorative objects—of unparalleled clarity. Steuben has enjoyed a loyal customer following; and its customers came along when it went to the Web, because the online user interface replicated as closely as possible the in-store customer experience. Luxury customers expect to find what they want easily: to facilitate a perfect experience, the site is

Box 6.1

THE AMAZING PEOPLE AT PRET A MANGER

Pret A Manger is a British sandwich shop that is far more than just a sandwich shop: It's a model of how a successful personal customer interface can rocket a company to the top of its category. Pret was founded by Julian Metcalfe and Sinclair Beecham, two London city workers who were dismayed by the lack of fresh lunch fare available in the area. Today there are 116 Pret stores in the U.K., several in Hong Kong, and a dozen in New York, and plans are underway to expand globally. Pret is so hot that McDonald's recently acquired a 33 percent share of the company, with a promise not to interfere in what makes Pret unique.

Just what does make Pret unique? Andrew Rolfe, Pret's Chairman and CEO, explains: "The Pret brand is about great-tasting, fresh, handmade, natural products served by people who are passionate about what they do."

To deliver a great interface experience, Pret needs what Andrew Rolfe calls "amazing people." It is not easy to become a part of the Pret team. In fact, Pret hires only 5 percent of those who apply. Job candidates have a general interview, then another interview with a local store manager. After that, they are sent to work for a day in a Pret shop. Employees who worked alongside the hopeful recruit are allowed to vote about whether the candidate should be hired. This process ensures good fit and good teamwork. An array of employee benefits—including incentive rewards, pay raises, company parties, and others—helps ensure the loyalty and happiness of Pret staffers.

Box 6.1   Continued

This unusual way of doing business extends to marketing. According to Morag McCay, Pret's marketing director, marketing at Pret equals "what we sell and why we sell it." In other words, Pret is not just selling sandwiches, it's selling the whole Pret platform. Customers have a right to expect integrity at every touchpoint with the company, and marketing campaigns are organized around the real truths of the company. In the words of Launa Williams, the company's communications manager, "we have never, ever sacrificed the quality of any product because it's very important to us and it reflects the brand and everything we do. There are a lot of important things that make Pret a success today: our people, our culture, and what we believe in."*

---

*Andy Milligan and Shaun Smith, *Uncommon Practice, Financial Times* (Upper Saddle River, NJ: Prentice-Hall, 2002), pp. 54–61.

---

deliberately shallow. Luxury buyers expect fast service: at the time of its launch, the site was blazingly fast—among the fastest on the Internet. Luxury buyers want their products in hand right away: the backend of the site was fully integrated with Steuben's existing ordering and inventory system, ensuring that online orders would be shipped out FedEx and usually reach the customer the next day.

The site was immediately successful, both with existing Steuben customers and with new buyers who became familiar with Steuben's offerings through the site. At one point during the height of the dot-com boom, the Steuben site was the fastest-growing revenue channel within Corning, with nearly 68 percent of its customers coming from the Web. Understanding customer expectations and paying scrupulous attention to the customer interface were key to this resounding success.

How Technology Improves the Interface Experience

As the Steuben case shows, the right interface should not only be staffed with the right people; it also must have the right technology. Technology can greatly improve the interface experience by putting the user in the driver's seat, by employing the right customer relationship management (CRM) programs, and by using technology to eliminate an inefficient interface.

Putting the User in the Driver's Seat

One of the best ways to use technology to improve an interface is to get customers to use the technology themselves.

Travel technology is a good example. Because more and more travelers are equipped with pagers, mobile phones, and PDAs, supplying travelers with the right wireless technology gives them greater control over their own travel experiences.

Several airlines have developed Internet and wireless technology that keep customers connected with them by providing accurate and timely information.

Proactive notification is an example. Airline customers can register on the Web site to get flight status information on a pager, mobile phone, or PDA including departure information, upgrades, and seat reservations. By specifying notification options (i.e., to which device and how often to provide information), the customer can customize the system. A spouse or friend can receive arrival information through either the Internet or another mobile device. Moreover, using the Web site, customers can download electronic timetables, request upgrades, review mileage accounts, shop for special Internet fares, and make reservations online or view them if they were made through other channels.

Employing Customized Relationship Programs

Another way of improving the customer experience is through customized relationship programs (CRPs). Imagine you have a friend who, in your mind, is one of your best friends; you run into her in the supermarket, and she does not recognize you. Imagine another friend with whom you had an evening-long dinner last night, and the next day he has forgotten that you went to dinner with him. Imagine yet another friend who tells you in the morning that she is willing to sell you her used car for $15,000; in the afternoon the price has gone up by 20 percent; and in the evening she decides to sell it to a mutual friend for half that price.

Friendships can take strange turns, but by any standards, none of the preceding situations would make for a lasting, stable, and intimate relationship. If you had any such encounters, you would probably conclude that your "friend" was schizophrenic, mean, or at best weird.

Yet, in business, we all have had such encounters with companies.

I have had credit card companies contact me and offer me a type of card that I already have. The staff at hotels where I have never previously stayed have greeted me with a smile and a "Welcome back." At a local store where I shop, newly hired bright-eyed salespeople often ask, "Sir, can I tell you about our delivery service?" when I have been using that delivery service for well over 10 years. We all have had similar encounters with companies that say that we are their friends, their loyal customers, their most valuable asset. Something is wrong with these relationships.

CRM programs were meant to fix such relationship problems by providing companies—via databanks and software—with an institutional memory about their customers similar to the everyday memory capacity that we expect from our best friends.[1] A CRM program like Hilton's, as discussed earlier, keeps track of all customer contacts for the customer's lifetime, and this information can help improve and personalize the customer experience.

A challenge for such programs in the future will be to enter inimitable, customized elements into customer's data fields, thus moving from CRM to CRPs. For example, the personnel of a hotel that I frequently visit may notice that I often turn up at the concierge desk and ask about the latest restaurant opening in the city. Before I embark on a trip, I would happily accept a personalized e-mail informing me about the latest restaurant openings in the city that I intend to visit. CRPs can play an important role in enhancing the interface experience.

Using Technology to Eliminate an Inefficient Interface

Not many salespeople are on the road these days selling encyclopedias. Fortunately so. In 1996, Encyclopedia Britannica canceled its door-to-door operations in favor of providing service over the Web. In July 2001, Britannica launched its online service and attracted 45,000 subscribers in the first year alone. Many computer users now realize that accurate information is available on the Internet and that they can access it and use it more efficiently than by searching through a book. Britannica has been able to use technological advances to eliminate an inefficient customer interface in favor of a more efficient and successful one.

Conclusion

The customer interface includes all kinds of exchanges between the company and customers in retail stores, by mail, phone, fax, online, and via instant messaging. As the dynamic contact between the customer and the company, the customer interface raises issues related to the right mix of essence and flexibility, style and substance, and the use of customers' time. To address these issues, companies need to attract and train the right staff and employ the right technology.

In addition to the brand experience and the customer interface, a company's innovativeness is another pillar of the customer experience. In Chapter 7, we discuss how engaging in continuous innovation is an imperative for an experience-oriented organization.

CHAPTER

7

Engaging in Continuous Innovation

To live up to the promise in its experiential platform, a company using CEM must engage in continuous innovation to enhance the customer experience and keep up with competition. This chapter explores how companies can create such innovations and describes successful ones that can serve as benchmarks for other companies.

From the CEM perspective, there are many different kinds of innovation. The "breakthrough product" refers to the new-to-the-world product that can change customer experiences entirely. Just think about the experience of ease and comfort that has come along with innovations in household appliances: washers and dryers, refrigerators and microwave ovens, vacuum cleaners, and air conditioners. Or think of milestone innovations that have allowed businesses to grow: the elevator, which enabled the modern office building; the escalator, which created the department store as we know it; the airplane, which facilitated global business; the computer, which changed how we work.

In addition to major breakthroughs, "small innovations" to existing products or the customer interface can enhance the customer experience. Innovation is at work in line extensions and brand extensions: the launch of a new flavor, the development of a new product form (e.g., liquid instead of powder detergent), or the use of an existing brand name in a new product category. In all these cases, relatively minor innovations may enrich the customer experience.

Finally, some marketing innovations reflect a company's superior creativeness in new product launches, special events, advertising and promotions, and other noticeable activities for its customers. In earlier chapters, we have already encountered several companies that have thrived on marketing innovations to enrich the customer experience: Jamba Juice (Chapter 4), Sephora (Chapter 5), and Nike (Chapter 6).

This chapter covers all these types of innovation and explains how to plan them to create the right customer experience. Before I present the key ideas and concepts, let's look at two cases. We will start with a company that returned to its innovation roots in the late 1990s and has excelled in the early years of the new century in practically all these aspects of innovation: Apple Computers. Apple has had breakthrough new products, line and brand extensions, and marketing innovation; and its track record in innovation has had a positive effect on how customers experience the company and its products. Next, we will look at experiential innovations at Amazon.com and how many small innovations can add up to a great customer experience.

Apple Computers: Returning to Its Innovation Roots

Apple has been known for its innovation for many years. When Apple hit hard times in the mid-1990s, its customers—some of the most loyal around—mourned what seemed to be the impending death of a company that had genuinely changed the way they lived their lives.

What saved Apple was, again, innovative spirit. In the late 1990s, the company returned to its roots and began creating products that profoundly affected the customer experience. Its great breakthrough innovation was the iMac, the affordable computer that lived up to Apple's advertising claims that buyers could get onto the Internet literally within 10 minutes of taking the computer out of the box. The iMac gave customers the ability to experience the Internet with unprecedented ease. And speed, too. Apple's G3 and G4 processors were the fastest in the world at the time of their introduction. A series of successful innovations that have followed the iMac—including the cool music appliance iPod, various laptop options, and DVD capabilities—set Apple clearly apart from its competitors.

Never a company to ignore details, Apple has also excelled at small innovations. As if the quantifiable benefits of the iMac weren't enough, Apple put its stamp on the product indelibly by creating an original line of five brightly colored translucent plastic cases, proving that computers can actually be attractive. Indeed, Apple unwittingly launched a major design trend with the iMac; even now, after Apple has abandoned its bright color palette, the trend for jewel-toned translucent cases thrives in everything from CD players to personal digital assistants (PDAs) to microwave ovens. Apple's influence has changed the customer experience even for customers who buy completely unrelated products.

Many companies would have been content to ride the wave of candy-colored computers indefinitely. Not Apple. It was already moving on to the next new innovation in iMacs: a stunning, space-age design featuring a podlike base and a flat screen that extends above the pod on a narrow stainless steel stem.

Apple's marketing innovations have been every bit as impressive as its product innovations. Its "Think Different" campaign attracted widespread attention and praise, and customers began to look forward to its playful ads for the iMac on billboards and bus stops everywhere. Apple showed that when the chips were down, it had the marketing savvy to get attention for its products.

Apple's innovative spirit permeates the whole company, and there are signs that different divisions of Apple share this spirit with one another. When Apple released the new version of its operating system, OS10.2, the marketing people seized on the project's developmental code name "Jaguar" and used it to brand the product: "Mac OS version 10.2 Jaguar." Continuing in this playful vein, Apple designed fur-print packaging and advertising with the clever tag line, "Wildly Innovative."

Amazon.com: Small Innovations Lead to a Great Online Experience

Since the beginning of its online life, Amazon.com has shown expertise at making small innovations add up to something big.

Just about everyone who has used Amazon.com realizes how great the site is. The online customer experience today is the result of continuous innovation based on adding features as technology has moved forward.

Amazon was one of the first Web sites to use cookies to customize the online experience. If you are a returning customer, Amazon.com greets you by name. Depending on your buying and browsing behavior on previous visits, the site offers recommendations to you: books, music, DVDs, kitchenware, and so on that are similar to items you have shopped for before. But say you already know what you are looking for . . . perhaps this book, *Customer Experience Management*. Type in the title in the search function and you are taken to the book's page, which makes it easy not only to buy it but also to browse around in similar titles and find out what other people think about the book. The page offers essential information about the book, including availability of copies in Amazon's warehouses. You know up front if the book is available to ship within 24 hours, 2 to 4 days, 3 weeks, whatever. No more of that horrible experience of placing an order—God forbid for a gift—and finding out a few days later the item is back-ordered and will be shipped "when available."

If you scroll down the page, you come to the "Great Buy" section, an innovative feature that offers the opportunity to buy this book along with another popular book on the same topic, at a discount. Directly below that is a panel headed "Customers Who Bought this Book Also Bought." The book titles listed there easily allow customers to note the range of books available on a particular topic.

Over the years, Amazon has gradually added more and more features that provide visitors with information about the items that interest them. In the "Product Details" section for a book, customers will find publishing information, the book's Amazon.com sales rank, the average customer review, and the various Amazon.com "Buyers Circle" groups where this book is selling well. By scrolling down the screen, you can see a selection of editorial reviews: Amazon's own review of the book, plus reviews from *Publisher's Weekly* and other major publications. Another special feature allows visitors to recommend another book in addition to—or instead of—the book currently being viewed. From the early days on, Amazon.com has encouraged user feedback and community development. Customer reviews are an important part of this policy. Anyone who is a registered user of Amazon can write a review of a book or other item. If you like, you can also provide information about yourself as a reviewer and create a page introducing yourself and listing all the reviews you have written. In this well-developed online community, customers can have a lively exchange of opinion about the books, music, and other items that they buy.

To approximate the in-store book-browsing experience, Amazon.com created the ingenious "Look Inside This Book" feature—customers can view actual pages from the printed book. This feature provides the closest possible online approximation of picking up the book in a bookstore and flipping through it. You can read the endorsements on the back cover, scan the table of contents and the index, and read a few pages to get the flavor of the writing.

Okay, now let's say you are convinced that this book is worthwhile; you are ready to buy. The Amazon.com interface makes purchase quick and easy. As a returning visitor, you have several options. An early innovation was the "One-Click" feature: if you so choose, the Amazon.com software can store all your buying information so you can avoid reentering it every time you want to make a purchase. Using your Amazon.com password, you can turn this feature on and off on all the computers you use, so that you can be sure your kids or coworkers are not making free with your credit card for their book and music purchases. Once you have placed your order, Amazon.com instantly sends an e-mail acknowledgment, and notifies you again when your order has shipped.

Amazon.com has developed as the capabilities of the Internet have grown, adding small innovations that have transformed the online customer experience. Amazon's ongoing innovations continue to shape what customers expect from a state-of-the-art online retailer.

How Innovation Contributes to Customer Experiences

As Apple and Amazon.com illustrate, innovation can contribute to customer experiences in several ways.

First, innovation increases the value of doing business with the company. This is particularly important for a computer manufacturer like Apple. Companies must create innovation on an ongoing basis (by offering new add-ons that can enhance the functions of the product or by offering new models with the same basic features as the current products). If they fail to do so, the existing products decrease in value for the customer, resulting in disappointing and frustrating experiences. That is exactly the feeling that many Apple customers experienced in the mid-1990s. The gap between a personal computer (PC) and an Apple was becoming narrower and narrower. In fact, in some categories such as laptops, PCs were gaining an edge in desirable customer features (e.g., weight, Internet connectivity, and portability). Some customers were afraid that Apple would go bankrupt. All these problems resulted from Apple's lack of innovation and caused a downward spiral; only after Steve Jobs returned to Apple in 1997 did its position improve. Nowadays, customer perceptions of Apple are entirely different. By regaining the innovative spirit that it first displayed in the early 1980s, Apple again can provide great value to its customers.

Second, innovation improves the lives of consumers and business customers by providing new solutions and thus new experiences. These solutions, though, do not remain new forever; other, newer solutions ultimately replace them. The marketing field has addressed this progression for many years through the concept of a "product life cycle." New products are introduced into the market, successful ones grow in the market until their sales reach maturity, and finally newer products replace them. Consider, for example, the move in business communication from letter writing to fax to e-mail and the corresponding changes in experiences in terms of immediacy of communication, ease, personalization, and intimacy. A company that can drive technology innovation adds tremendous experiential value by improving people's lives.

Some Japanese companies have shown experiential innovation in a realm that receives little attention in the West: the toilet. In the hands of Japanese engineers, the lowly toilet has become both a comfort aid and a health-management tool.

Because of the country's dense population, the bathroom may be the only room in the average Japanese household where a person can find real privacy. Toilet manufacturers are working to enhance that experience. Matsushita, for example, has developed a $3,000 toilet seat that includes a heating and cooling unit. When a person enters the room, the toilet automatically raises its seat and commences adjusting the temperture. The user can pre-program the unit to heat or air-condition the room at a specific time each day. According to Hiroyuki Matsui, the company's chief engineer, "you can bring a bathroom temperature down by 7 degrees Celsius in 30 seconds."[1]

Inax, a rival company, offers a toilet that can play six soundtracks, including chirping birds, rushing water, ringing wind-chimes, or a traditional Japanese harp.

Product developers are also working hard to develop the health-related potential of the toilet. Toto, a major player in the market, offers a model called the WellyouII, a toilet that uses a small retractable spoon to capture urine and measure the user's urine sugar level. Matsushita has ambitious plans for an Internet-linked toilet that can use a phone connection to feed a variety of health data to the user's doctor, including weight, body fat, blood pressure, urine sugar, albumin, and blood in the urine. Developers expect this model to be a reality within five years, and with Japan's aging population, it could be seen as a highly practical device.

Finally, innovation can project an image of relevance. When a company is no longer seen as relevant, it loses customers. Even though it may produce serviceable products, it will acquire the image of being old-fashioned and stuck in the past. Sooner or later, its customers will migrate toward competitors that display an innovative approach. Amazon.com, through continuous innovation in its interface, has remained relevant to customers.

The Gap faced such an innovation challenge in the early years of the new century. The company was no longer seen as relevant, having alienated its baby-boomer customers with beaded, hip-hugging, belly-baring styles that failed to attract even the youth market. Its fashions seemed out of touch with the desired customer experience of any target segment. The company had built its name on khakis, white T-shirts, jeans, and other basics that were right on the mark in the 1990s as the casual workplace grew in popularity. When Sharon Stone wore a $25 black Gap top at the 1996 Academy Awards, The Gap became the darling of Wall Street. In the early years of the new century, however, the product line—along with the product lines of its Old Navy and Banana Republic brands—was seen as increasingly irrelevant. As stressed earlier, innovation involves not only product but also marketing innovation. In that respect, The Gap also seemed tired. There was a drought of several years during which there was not a single notable ad campaign or product display like the clever "Khakis Swing" or Old Navy's vegetable-counter-inspired packaging of T-Shirts. In February 2002, the stock, which had hit a high of $53 in February 2000, was trading at $12. Its CEO, Millard Drexler, resigned after reporting a $34 million fourth quarter loss for fall 2001.

Customer Experience and Innovation Strategy

I highly recommend that a company incorporate the customer experience into its innovation strategy and plan. Because innovation affects the customer experience in significant ways, companies need to capture the customer experience early on and then include it in new development and marketing efforts. This will guide the company in selecting the innovations it should pursue in the years to come. Moreover, experience-driven innovation needs to be related to the company's experiential platform.

A company that uses monolithic branding by calling all its products by the company name (as many industrial companies do) is more likely to benefit from such an approach than a company that is essentially a holding company of different brands (like Procter & Gamble). In the latter case, customers still may get many of the benefits resulting from the firm's innovativeness, but they may not associate it with one company.

The innovation plan should not be too narrow because it may limit the company in seeking new opportunities. It should, however, guide decision making internally and externally. At minimum, the company needs to decide whether it will provide experiential innovations primarily through major breakthroughs, small innovations, or marketing innovations. In addition, it may be helpful to specify the applications or product category where innovation is likely and the general form it may take. Apple innovations, for example, are always about design and usability, characteristics that are in line with Apple's experiential platform.

Experience and New Product Development

Since a desirable customer experience must be the ultimate goal of a business, a company seeking breakthrough innovation should incorporate the customer experience into the product development process. Sound like *Mission Impossible?* In many companies, it is. Most R&D departments are inhabited by engineers and technicians who tend to ignore input from customers, especially from focus groups commissioned by the marketing department.

"The engineers and technicians have a point," you may say. "They may be right in taking the lead and trusting their expertise and their instincts. Does it make sense to believe that customers could envision radical innovations and provide useful feedback in the development of really new products?"

Certainly, customer input is not always helpful, especially when it comes to technical intricacies. Asking customers to imagine a not-well-thought-out product or talking about general innovation in a conventional focus group is likely to be a waste of time. However, once the company has a clear idea and perhaps even a prototype, it should definitely be tested with customers in an experiential way.

I have consulted and conducted workshops on how to incorporate experience into the new product development on several occasions. Many companies that have quantified success and failure of their new products have observed that products are more successful when the company seeks customer input early on in the development process. Conversely, product failures are often the result of misunderstanding what customers want.

Lycra Soft, a "shaping garment" that offered women comfortable everyday underwear with the added benefit of shaping their bodies, was not as successful as planned when it launched in 1996. The product failed because it did not provide the right experience: it was so comfortable that women believed it had no effect and as a result they did not feel thinner or better shaped than without it.

A better understanding of the customer experience—how women relate to their bodies—might have helped DuPont's product development and marketing team better reach its target customers.

How can the customer experience be included early on in the development process? Imagine that you are a manufacturer of mobile phones and PDAs; development then requires an understanding of how people will use these products. How are people moving about; are they playing sports when they use the products; do they put them in a jacket or on a belt; do they bump into things; how should these products fit into and complement customers' experiences?

As part of the market-assessment phase of the new product development process, most companies conduct broad-based life-cycle studies, competitive analyses, and product portfolio analyses. At this first stage of product development, however, they rarely strive to understand the experiential world of the customer.

Experience at Various Stages of Product Development

The first column of Figure 7.1 displays the typical stages of the new product development process that many companies use.

< 1 > market assessment
analyzing the experiential world of the customer

< 2 > idea generation
generating experiential solutions

< 3 > concept testing
testing the experiential appeal of the concept

< 4 > product design
incorporating the experience in product specification

< 5 > product testing
testing the customer's usage experience

FIGURE 7.1
The CEM Approach for the Five Steps of New Product Development

Presented alongside is the experiential approach to new product development for each stage.

Incorporating the experience *throughout* the new product development process is an exciting, customer-driven proposition. To achieve this objective, it is essential to understand the experiential world of the customer and to include design prototypes in the research at different stages of the new product's development. Moreover, the design team must be open to suggestions from customers and must be creative in developing appropriate applications and solutions.

To include experience into the development of a portable electronic product (a mobile phone, PDA, or other portable digital device), developers might use the following six-stage process:

1. Do a broad-based conceptual and empirical analysis of the experiential world of the customer (using innovative, real-life research techniques with visual and multimedia displays).

2. Develop and test broad-based graphic style options related to the customer's desires for the electronics product.

3. Gain an understanding of specific functional options for the product that relate to specific and desirable customer experiences and lifestyles.

4. Develop and test broad-based design prototypes for the product with key functional features.

5. Develop and test specific experiential options in a product prototype.

6. Conduct a usability study in people's natural environment (multiple situations related to target lifestyles) and fine-tune the design.

This process is somewhat iterative, moving customer input to the design team and vice versa. Moreover, experiential measurement techniques should be used in the project. To capture experience, three sets of measures could be used:

1. Measures related to the functionality and usability of the product that have experiential appeal in different usage situations.

2. Measures related to the overall feeling toward the product.

3. Measures related to the specific experiential impact on senses, feelings, thinking, acting, and relating (similar to the EX Scale mentioned in Chapters 1 and 5).

Box 7.1

SONY: FROM FREQ OUT TO PSYC OUT

Right at the turn of the millennium, Sony Electronics launched a successful Walkman cassette and radio player wrapped in a translucent plastic enclosure with a unique graphical treatment. Sony designers developed the products in collaboration with Jaeger DePaulo Kemp, a graphics design consultancy in Burlington, Vermont, using the experiential concepts that I developed. The company also conducted massive research on the young target group's experience including observations of skateboarders and the skateboard culture, name testing to select a name that related to the lingo of the target audience, and focus groups with 10- and 12-year-olds. The final product had a flexible plastic exoskeleton that shielded the product from hard bumps and allowed the player to suspend it from a belt. A generic cassette and radio player was thus reborn as a sassy Gen-Y playing device. After the success of the first line (it gained around 6 share points in this very mature market), dozens of second-generation models for Discman and Walkman radio products and headphones were launched under the label "Psyc." Pronounced "Sike," the term is short for "psychology" and has associations with the teen parlance of "psyching someone out." Within Sony, it is an acronym for Products Signifying Youth Culture. These products had bright colors, translucent plastics with psychedelic swirls and geometric buttons, new bumper design, and touch-sensitive surfaces that left a telltale impression after the user had handled the product.

These measures should be in part verbal and in part based on input using multisensory stimuli. Part of the measurement could be a scale and part of it a scorecard to help evaluate the innovation progress.

Experience and Small Innovations

As mentioned, innovation does not have to be all break-through, new-to-the-world innovation and R&D intensive. Small innovations in line and brand extensions or new products can improve the experience nonetheless.

In Chapter 3, I described how tracking customer touch-points along the decision-making process could deliver a better experience. These ideas can be used as well to develop a lot of small innovations that improve the customer experience. Consider the moviegoing experience along some key decision steps:

- *Decision making.* Placing trailers on Internet sites that customers can view on their computers can experientially facilitate their movie choices.
- *Purchase.* Making phone or Internet reservations can eliminate the annoying experience of standing in line for tickets when the movie may already be starting.
- *Consumption.* Comfortable seats, oversized screens, digital sound systems, and the policy of asking visitors to turn off their mobile phones can greatly improve the experience.

AMC, a company that owns movie theaters across the United States, has created such small innovations in the moviegoing experience. As stated in AMC's 2001 Annual Report, "We anticipated the demand of a superior moviegoing experience, and committed early to a megaplex strategy." This strategy included the construction of more than 10,000 new movie screens from 1995 to 2000, with 83 percent of screens located in the 25 largest markets in the United States and international screens located in key European and Pacific Rim markets.

A megaplex is a multitheater complex offering a range of services besides movies. One such complex that opened in 2002 in Dallas, Texas, includes 24 theaters that can seat 4,400 moviegoers. It also has a soft play area for children, specialty shops, and restaurants. Enhancements of the moviegoing experience include stadium seating, wall-to-wall movie screens, superior sight and sound, cupholder armrests, and AMC's trademarked "LoveSeats" that contour to the body and offer lumbar support. Convenient pre-theater services include movietickets.com, an Internet ticketing service, and MovieWatcher, a trademarked frequent moviegoer program that rewards consumers with free popcorn and soft drinks, as well as season passes.

Experience and Marketing Innovation

The goal of marketing innovation is to create a big splash in the marketplace through unusual communications, special events, or other marketing ventures.

You know that you have achieved a marketing innovation when the customer says, "Wow." Marketing innovations are surprising, intriguing, and often a little bit provocative. They result from thinking out-of-the box, having guts, and taking risks.

Event marketing (e.g., trade shows, road shows, and sponsorships) is an example of marketing innovation. According to a study that Intellitrends conducted in late 2001, event marketing, especially if done creatively, provides a better return on investment (ROI) of marketing spending than advertising, sales promotion, or public relations.[2]

"Brand celebrations" are another example of marketing innovation. Some magazines have a special issue every year to celebrate their birthday. Even better are the innovative, big-scale marketing spectaculars that companies stage to celebrate the brand anniversary. They are ways of connecting with customers and can also be an internal morale boost. In 2001, Indian Motorcycles celebrated its one-hundredth anniversary with a 5,300-mile Centennial Ride from Springfield, Massachusetts, site of the original Indian Motorcycles factory to Gilroy, California, site of the current factory. Riders included the top management team, as well as factory leaders. During the two-week ride, riders stopped at various Indian Motorcycles dealerships across the country.

Many companies miss opportunities to make a big splash at anniversaries. When a composer's hundredth birthday comes around, a flurry of activities frequently commemorate this birthday. When brands have special birthdays, however, companies are often highly unoriginal in planning celebrations.

Once we involve others in spreading the innovation, we have a buzz campaign. To turn a "wow" marketing idea into "buzz" requires that the idea be unusual, that it can be shared, and that it be "shareworthy." According to *BusinessWeek*, this is how buzz works:

Frequent the right cafes in Sunset Plaza, Melrose, or the Third Street Promenade in and around Los Angeles this summer, and you're likely to encounter a gang of sleek, impossibly attractive motorbike riders who seem genuinely interested in getting to know you over an iced latte. Compliment them on their Vespa scooters glinting in the brilliant curbside sunlight, and they'll happily pull out a pad and scribble down an address and phone number—not theirs, but that of the local "boutique" where you can buy your own Vespa, just as (they'll confide) the rap artist Sisqó and the movie queen Sandra Bullock recently did. That's when the truth hits you: This isn't any spontaneous encounter. Those scooter-riding models are on the Vespa payroll, and they've been hired to generate some favorable word of mouth for the recently reissued European bikes.[3]

Buzz is a hot trend—and not just in California. Buzz has been used to explain the success of all sorts of products among consumers, from Razor Scooters to Harry Potter and low-budget cult movies like *The Blair Witch Project*. Within a few years, it moved from a fringe, underground technique into the mainstream. According to industry reports, every major brand from the staid (Ford, P&G, General Electric) to the hip (Nike, Palm, PowerBar) uses it. Two of the reasons: buzz is cost-effective, and it attracts attention.

As a concept and practice, however, it has an even more exciting aspect. It is a creative technique that falls outside the realms of traditional company-controlled strategic management and communications: once seeded, it takes on its own dynamic and spreads like a virus.

Emanuel Rosen, author of *The Anatomy of Buzz*, defines buzz as "the sum of all comments that are exchanged among people at a given time."[4] The customer owns buzz. This is the most important aspect of buzz marketing. Customers are more skeptical than ever about company communications that use mass media advertising. They seem to trust their friends, however. According to a 2001 report by consulting firm McKinsey & Company, word of mouth influences 67 percent of U.S. consumer goods sales.

Buzz can also significantly increase the value of a company. Many small companies have parlayed the buzz they have generated into lucrative acquisition deals: Samantha by Coca-Cola, Snapple by Pepsi, and Crème de la Mer by Estee Lauder, to name just a few.

A word of caution is in order, however. Although buzz is an exciting new development in marketing, it runs the risk of manipulating the customer deceptively (e.g., with fake personal phone numbers). Buzz must be done right; it is most effective when it allows customers to create an experience community. This requires that the product or message be worth propagating and that other creative initiatives keep buzz alive.

Conclusion

The last component of the implementation of the CEM framework is innovation. It includes any improvement to the customer experience whether it results from breakthrough new products, small innovations, or marketing innovations. Engaging in continuous innovation requires a forward-looking process and management approach. Unlike continuous improvement or

---

Box 7.2

THE MINI IS BACK

In the late 1990s, Volkswagen brought back the New Beetle, the turn-of-the millennium reincarnation of a 1960s classic. I am pleased to report that the "retro" innovation goes on, with the rebirth of yet another classic car that sparked the imagination of a generation: the Mini Cooper.

In 1958, designer Alec Issigonis created the first Mini, a small family sedan with room for four adults, that could also be driven like a sports car. The Mini became an icon for the swinging 60s in Britain, boasting among its owners comedian

Showroom design by Plajer & Franz studio. Photography by Friedrich Busam.

(continued)

Box 7.2 Continued

Peter Sellers and assorted Beatles. The "S" version of Rover's Mini dominated the Monte Carlo rally during the 1960s.

Forty years passed, the British automotive industry fell on hard times, and virtually no changes were made to the Mini until BMW purchased Rover and poured money into revamping the classic. The results have been stunning. The new Mini Cooper honors the design ethos of the original, with its wheel-at-each-corner construction and low center of gravity. But the innovations have made it a safer and more powerful machine. The BMW version is larger than its ancestor and about a thousand pounds heavier. Its assembly has been described as "jewel-like," its interior like "something Picasso might have conjured on a wine-enlivened Saturday night." Minis come in a variety of colors, with a distinctive white or black roof. At $16,850, car enthusiasts in the U.S. and elsewhere are snapping them up.

---

kaizen—a hot management idea from Japan in the late 1980s and early 1990s, experience-driven innovation is not product or operation focused. In line with the CEM philosophy, it is a truly customer-oriented process that seeks to incorporate the customer experience into R&D and marketing to produce improvements at all customer touchpoints.

CHAPTER 8

Delivering a Seamlessly Integrated Customer Experience

As we have seen, CEM provides a step-by-step framework for managing the customer experience. But it is more than that. It is also an integrative management approach for delivering a seamlessly integrated experience to the customer, not a piecemeal one. The framework is successful only if the customer perceives an experience as a unified whole instead of a point-by-point delivery of random impressions. This chapter shows how to achieve CEM's overarching goal of seamless integration.

The term "integration" has become a popular buzzword in management and marketing, frequently used without any concern for what it can actually achieve. The strategic management concepts of vertical and horizontal integration are really nothing more than operational concepts focused on economic efficiencies ("cost savings" and "economies of scale") or vague strategy statements ("synergies" and "strategic alignment"). There is nothing concrete about these terms: no concept or methodology to define how and under what conditions managers should pursue this integration. Not surprisingly, mergers and acquisitions alternate every few years with spin-off and sell-off activities that result in disintegration, and send companies back to square one.

"Integrated marketing communications" is not much better. Here, too, the focus has been operational (on saving communication costs) or broadly strategic (on conveying a unified brand image). Again, what is missing is specificity: How do managers plan and deliver such communication integration? And what are the concepts and methodologies that can help marketers get it done?

In the CEM framework, integration is far more than a buzzword. It is an approach that is anchored in a rich set of practical ideas and management tools. In this chapter, we look at various levels of integration, and examine how you can integrate the customer experience across all touchpoints.

The Power of Integration

Seamless integration has three key benefits:

1. *Integration provides differentiation.* Because integration is rarely done well and is so different from most business

campaigns, it is extremely attention getting. It is impressive to see that a company has made the effort of "bringing it all together" for the customer.

2. *Integration provides deep connection with customers.* Integration engages customers intellectually and emotionally. It includes novel and surprising ways of connecting with customers and thus provides a memorable experience that is worth sharing.

3. *Integration saves costs.* When using an integrative approach to connect with customers, the company speaks with one voice and does not dissipate communicative impact in communication clutter. For small or medium-sized firms or those with limited budgets, integration can be a cost-effective way to achieve the same impact as that of a larger, but less connected, campaign. More important, having a small budget forces managers to spend the money carefully and creatively; integration is an ideal way to get the company's message across.

I have worked with several clients on integrating the customer experience. To be successful, a company must employ the powerful tool of integration at different levels.

First, analysis, strategy, and implementation must be integrated in a seamless way. A customer-focused analysis needs to lead to a relevant experiential positioning and value promise to the key target segment. This positioning and EVP must result in an overall implementation theme that is being delivered through the product, through the communications, in the store, and during the launch events.

191

Moreover, the company must deliver integration within an implementation domain—whether it is the brand experience, the interface, or continuous innovation—and show how integration within a domain can benefit the customer and the company. Elements of the brand experience (advertising, public relations, and the store design) must be brought together to deliver one clear, integrated communication message. Elements of the customer interface (the salespeople, the informational aspects of the Web site as well as other customer contacts) must be structured to provide unified and integrated service. Finally, in the case of a new product launch, an innovative product, teaser campaign, and launch event must convey to the customer that the company engages in an integrated innovation effort.

Most important, the company needs to show how to connect the brand experience with the interface, the interface with innovation, and innovation with the brand experience to provide integration across all domains.

Let's take a closer look at how a company can accomplish the three levels of integration. I will refer to them as "strategic integration from top to toe," "integration within implementation domains," and "integration across implementation domains" (see Figure 8.1). The following concepts and methodologies will allow you to use integration as a powerful management tool to connect with your customers.

Strategic Integration from Head to Toe

Integration through the five steps of a CEM project achieves strategic integration from head to toe. Think of it this way:

strategic integration from head to toe

✳ linking analysis, strategy and implementation

integration within implementation domains

✳ signatures

✳ domain themes

integration across implementation domains

✳ linkages

FIGURE 8.1

Three Types of CEM Integration

your customer does not have access to the analysis and strategy phase. The brain, or the "head" of your CEM project consists of analysis and strategy, but they are hidden from the customer. What the customer sees and gets is the brand experience, the interface, and your innovations. These visible manifestations are the body of your strategy—all the way to the smallest detail—all the way to the little toe. Through these implementation domains, you express the quality of your analysis and strategy. That is where you need to create the image of your company or brand. That is where you need to deliver on the experiential value promise (EVP). That is where you need to bring the overall implementation theme to life.

Several features of the CEM framework ensure that you can achieve strategic integration from head to toe:

- Conceptually, the CEM framework has one origin. There is a genuine customer focus throughout the framework (see Chapter 2); there are numerous, linked customer-focused concepts and ideas within each step (see Chapters 3 through 7); and one step follows naturally from the other. In contrast, many marketing strategies and strategic management frameworks are a hodgepodge of theories in economics, sociology, psychology, and military strategy, combined with a heavy dose of metaphors and anecdotes that try to pass as "common sense." Such frameworks provide inept strategic integration. That is why, as mentioned in Chapter 1, many managers are disappointed that the implementation often does not express the strategy.

- Operationally, there are several "bridging concepts" between the five steps. Consider the bridging concepts in Step 2 ("the experiential platform") and how they project backward to Step 1 and forward to Steps 3, 4, and 5. The analysis of the experiential world is used to formulate positioning options. The EVP is used to specify types of experience (*Sense, Feel, Think, Act, Relate*) that can be created by managing the brand, the interface, and innovations. Finally, the overall implementation theme specifies style and content: the overall implementation theme guides how and what the company wants to communicate about itself and its brands.

- Methodologically, the research techniques of the CEM framework can be used at various steps and thus provide further

194

continuity and strategic integration. Natural habitat research can be used for understanding how customers experience their daily lives, for designing experiential positioning options, for testing a store design or a store interface, and for idea generation in new product development.

Yet it is not enough just to have a framework that enables strategic integration conceptually, operationally, and methodologically. Strategic integration may fail because of the way the company thinks, how it is organized, and how it consequently manages an experience project.

For an experience project to succeed, it is important to get everyone on board and make sure that they are focusing on the customer experience. This can be a difficult task in engineering- or sales-focused organizations. Moreover, everybody must know what everybody else is doing and take that knowledge into account when planning and executing any part of the project.

Integration requires a shift in thinking as well as employee involvement and ownership of key initiatives. Also needed is a driving force behind the strategic integration—be it an "integration champion," a committee that takes charge, or an outside consultancy that specializes in it. No matter who does it, somebody must bring about an integrated analysis, strategy, and implementation.

Finally, over time, a company that is serious about managing the customer experience must develop continuous capabilities in managing the three implementation domains: the brand, the interface, and innovations. The capabilities include experiential marketing, experience-driven human resource practices and technologies, and corporate creativity. Chapter 9 provides details about these essential capabilities.

Integration *within* Implementation Domains

In the preceding three chapters, we focused on the implementation domains of the CEM framework: the brand, the interface, and innovations. Each domain has specific implementation elements that deliver the experience. They are the "experience providers," a concept I introduced in my book *Experiential Marketing*. Here are some experience providers for the implementation domains:

- For the brand experience: the company or brand name and the logo, ads, store design, and the Web design.
- For the interface: interactions with salespeople, a chat session on the Internet, and a personal sales call.
- For innovations: new goods, new services, line extensions, brand extensions, and new buzz campaigns.

In the CEM approach, it is paramount to integrate these diverse elements. There are two techniques for doing so.

The first technique is direct. The company develops a "signature" that is associated with all the elements within a domain. For example, when designing the brand experience, we create a visual brand signature that appears in, or is associated with, all brand elements (the logo, the store, the ads, the Web site). It may consist of certain icons and graphic designs (e.g., colors, shapes, icons, symbols). Or, for the customer interface, the signature may be certain consistent greetings of the customer (e.g., the greeter uses the customer's first name and adds a friendly "Hello. How are you? We are glad to serve you again today"), each time the customer appears in a store, purchases on the Web, or receives direct mail. Finally, for innovations, the signature may be a consistent way of launching and marketing new products.

A more sophisticated technique is to develop a domain theme that is similar to, but more specific than, the overall implementation theme. It should relate precisely to all the elements of a given implementation domain—a brand theme, an interface theme, an innovation theme, so to speak.

Burton Snowboards, one of the most successful sellers of snowboards, uses as its overall implementation theme "community and fun for all riders." The brand experience brings this overall implementation theme to life through dynamic, attention-getting graphic design elements. All brand communications and the online Web magazine, www.snowboardermag .com, follow this brand theme. Everywhere there is thrilling photography of incredible jumps; vibrant and unusual graphics; and event sponsorships and co-branding with other exciting companies.

An example of an interface theme is the employee behavior and the treatment that customers receive when they stay at a W hotel. The theme may be characterized as casual, cool, yet friendly service, and it is implemented throughout the hotel. The front-desk personnel wear black and behave professionally but casually; the telephone operator is called for "whatever, whenever" and uses this phrase as a greeting; and the concierge, the bartenders, even the valet can recommend all sorts of cool places.

A theme can be developed even for innovations. General Electric's famous "We bring good things to life" can be seen as an innovation theme, not just an advertising slogan, because the company uses it to communicate the innovations that it has produced over many decades and will produce in the future.

The General Electric example demonstrates that such themes can provide not only coherence among implementation elements but also consistency of the experience over time. Absolut Vodka has been successful in providing such consistency with its brand theme. It portrays the Absolut bottle in creative and funky ways as being related to all sorts of things in the world, whether it is in advertising, outdoor installations, or on the Web. In 2002, with 60 percent market share, the brand was the market leader in the United States in the imported vodka category of more than 150 brands. When Seagram's, the distributor of the brand, sold its distribution rights in 2001, the brand accounted for about one-third of the profitability of Seagram's entire liquor division. A well-developed theme, and a consistent brand experience in turn, can cut through communication clutter, create an icon in the marketplace, and be a huge moneymaking machine for the brand owners.

What we have discussed thus far are two forms of integration—seamless integration from analysis to strategy to implementation, and integration *within* implementation domains. What makes the CEM approach particularly appealing and innovative, however, is a third, higher-level integration that links the three implementation domains (brand experience, interface, and innovation) in a creative and sophisticated manner.

198

Integration *across* Implementation Domains

Providing integration across implementation domains is more complex than accomplishing the forms of integration previously discussed. This is because implementing the customer experience in a given domain requires specific training and expertise. The implementation of the brand experience requires the expertise of the marketing department internally and the so-called creative professions externally: advertising, graphic design, Web design, and so on. Most of these firms employ people with arts and literature degrees, though you may also find a couple of people with MBAs, who manage the accounts. The human resource function manages the customer interface internally, perhaps in conjunction with some service consultants. Innovation is the domain of R&D and, insofar as it involves marketing innovation, of the marketing department and event management firms.

The different professions have their own concepts, ideas, and stereotypes about each other, which can make it difficult for them to work together smoothly. Trying to break down these stereotypes can be difficult and time-consuming. A more promising and faster approach is to use a powerful management concept and technique in a collaborative context that avoids stereotypes and gets people to work together.

The top-level concept and technique for integration across domains is "providing linkages." Linkages are different from the signatures and themes that you can use for integration within domains. Linkages utilize two domains at the same time, or even all three, to engage and connect with the customer in creative and unusual ways.

Imagine, for example, you are opening a stand-alone store for one of your brands. Rather than just using the store as a selling space, you could think of it as a stage for innovative events, performances, and sales promotions to celebrate the experiential platform of your brand. These events, performances, and promotions may include—a fashion show, a talk show, a music performance, a scientific lecture, a disco party, or whatever may fit the brand. In all of them, the brand could be present, and be sold. As part of an innovative teaser campaign, you could use the space even before the store formally opens, as some museums and art galleries have done before the opening of a show. You can employ the space to reach out to neighboring communities and to the innovators of your target segment. You could feature some of the events as part of your advertising and PR campaign. You can develop innovative add-on products that remind your customers of the brand and the staged events. Most important, you can do all this by paying much less and having higher impact than if you engage in a traditional store launch.

The following examples demonstrate linkages in detail (see Figure 8.2).

Linkages between the Brand and the Interface

"Experiential promotions" can provide linkages between the brand experience and the customer interface. These are promotional events in the store, on the Web, or at any other interface that provides a link to the brand experience. These are not price discounts; instead, they use an experiential feature of the brand and play with it. For example, Jamba Juice could run a promotion with its Energy Boost through which

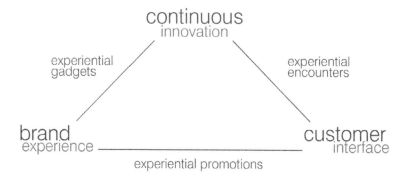

FIGURE 8.2

Examples of Linkages

customers might win a free trip to the place where "mind and body energy" meet—such as China, the birthplace of Gingko Biloba and other energy-producing vitamins and minerals. Or for a hotel chain, it might be an unexpected freebie such as the cake that magically appears in your room on your birthday.

Customers love indulging in hedonic pleasures and clearly prefer experiential rewards to monetary ones. My colleagues at Columbia Business School, Ran Kivetz and Itamar Simonson, have done extensive research to prove this point.[1] They intercept customers at shopping malls and ask them whether they would prefer a monetary award for a certain service that they provide to the researcher or a hedonic award at the same monetary value or even less (e.g., a trip on a cruise ship or a spa treatment). In numerous studies, Kivetz has shown that customers prefer the hedonic award that provides an experience to the monetary one. From a classic economic perspective, such behavior makes no sense: money allows for planning and for more choice, including the choice of buying the hedonic award. On the other hand, we can all relate to customers' preference for the tangible experience. It's awfully human, isn't it?

Linkages between the Brand and Innovation

These linkages are what I call "experiential gadgets." They are products that are new to the company or brand and that exist solely to reinforce the brand experience. In and of themselves, these gadgets are not expected to become big-selling items, although they can provide buzz and sometimes turn into a profitable business on their own.

Many fashion and cosmetics brands have discovered that specially scented and flavored candles and water are effective experiential gadgets for reinforcing the brand experience of the lifestyle fashion or cosmetics brands. Jazz CDs at Starbucks or CDs with romantic themes at Victoria's Secret are experiential gadgets. Selling experiential gadgets for cars (key chains, sunglasses, ties, or miniature models of the cars) is a highly successful business.

Product variety can be used as an "experiential gadget" and create huge buzz. In the spring of 2002, M&M Mars, the creator of the ever-popular M&M's candy, launched a massive, global customer feedback campaign to select a new candy color to include in the regular pack of M&M's. A similar campaign was run in 1995, leading to the advent of the blue M&M (blue replaced tan, which in turn had replaced violet in 1948). Candy fans had two months to cast their votes via the Internet and regular mail. In the end, 41 percent of respondents voted for purple over its opponents, aqua and pink, so in July M&M Mars announced that purple would indeed be the new color. Over 10 million people participated in the polling worldwide, a stunning opportunity for M&M Mars to interact with its customers. The company has even come up with a way for the "losers" to win: candy lovers who want M&M's in nonstandard colors can simply visit the M&M's Web site, go to the Colorworks section, and customize their own candy order from a selection of 21 colors.

Linkages between the Interface and Innovation

To create linkages between the interface and innovation, the company must provide what I call "experiential encounters" that are dynamic, interactive, and innovative.

For example, the company may create interactive offers as part of sponsorship or co-op events (e.g., NTT DoCoMo's involvement at NikePark Tokyo, discussed in Chapter 6). Or the company may organize annual customer events such as the open-house reunions of Harley-Davidson, Saturn, BMW, and other companies. Moreover, starting in the mid-1990s, the Internet and e-commerce provided new experiential encounters, not only for B2C commerce but also for B2B commerce through online markets and auctions. In the years to come, communication and commerce via digital mobile devices such as mobile phones will provide new personalized experiential encounters between a firm and its customers.

Experiential encounters are superb ways to connect with customers and receive valuable information from them. In that sense, they can even be used as yet another sophisticated "natural habitat" research technique.

Conclusion

Integration is a powerful tool that must occur at various levels: from analysis through strategy to implementation, *within* as well as *across* implementations. However, integration does not just occur when companies have the right ideas and techniques. Like all of customer experience management, integration is not just a cognitive management tool. To really accomplish integration within an organization, management must meet certain organizational requirements. In the final chapter, we discuss these organizational requirements and look at the complete CEM model for delivering a profitable customer experience.

9

Organizing for Customer Experience Management

Now that you have the framework for managing a CEM project and for integrating the experience across all customer touchpoints, you need to explore one more area: the organizational alignment necessary to support CEM. Based on viewing customers as its key financial assets, the company must invest in the customer experience to derive a financial return. To do so, the company needs to employ internal resources that it allocates to CEM. Moreover, the company needs to treat its own employees as customers who desire a positive experience.

Organizing for CEM thus includes three tasks:

1. *Financial planning of CEM in terms of customers.* CEM's ultimate goal is a fair and mutually beneficial long-term business relationship between the company and its customers. Because using the company's goods and services helps customers lead more rewarding personal or business lives, they will in turn reward the company financially by doing business with it, being loyal, and, over time, bringing in new business. The value of the customer to the firm, referred to as *customer equity,* will increase, and the company will grow and be profitable. Customers, therefore, are assets that the company invests in through CEM and from which it can expect a return on its investment (ROI). To engage in financial planning around this investment in customers, the company must develop a model that shows how improving the customer experience can impact customer equity.

2. *Allocation of organizational resources.* Improving the customer experience, and thus increasing customer equity, requires internal resources. The company needs to ask what financial, structural, and personnel resources it needs to engage in CEM to deliver an ongoing desirable experience to customers. Resources must be allocated to each of the three implementation domains of the customer experience discussed earlier in the book: the brand experience, the customer interface, and innovation.

3. *Enhancement of the employee experience.* The concept of experience applies not only to *external customers* but also to *internal customers,* that is, the company's employees. Applying CEM to human resource management involves

more than just tweaking a few procedures. Instead, CEM represents a whole new HR philosophy that goes far beyond the standard practices of offering employees greater control, more challenging work, more teamwork, and better compensation. What all employees, across all levels, get from an experience-oriented organization is a more rewarding *employee experience* that includes a new form of professional and personal development. Employees of such an organization live a more experiential and thus more satisfying and productive life. They are also more motivated and capable of delivering a great experience to customers.

In this final chapter, I focus on these three broad organizational themes and tasks: defining and quantifying the relation between customer experience and customer equity, allocating organizational resources, and enhancing the employee experience.

The *complete CEM model* shows how internal resources affect the customer experience and how the customer experience in turn provides financial for the firm (see Figure 9.1). How does this model differ from the CEM framework discussed in previous chapters? Both the CEM framework and the complete CEM model are key management tools. The framework is a step-by-step navigation device for conducting a CEM project, with pertinent concepts and methodologies. The complete CEM model allows you to define and quantify empirical relations between the customer experience with tangible outcome measures and with organizational requirements. With its metrics, you can

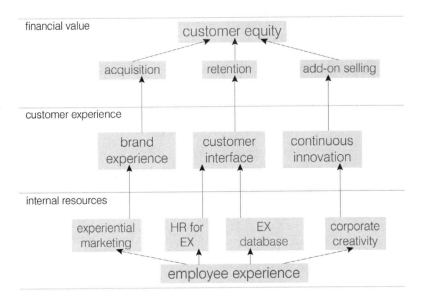

financial value

customer equity

acquisition   retention   add-on selling

customer experience

brand experience   customer interface   continuous innovation

internal resources

experiential marketing   HR for EX   EX database   corporate creativity

employee experience

FIGURE 9.1
The Complete CEM Model

treat the model as a scorecard. You can pinpoint where things go right, where they need improvement, and what returns to expect from your investment in CEM. The model will help you make informed decisions about investments, personnel, and technology.

At the top of the model is one of the key terms of this chapter, customer equity. I begin by defining customer equity and discussing its components. Then I consider how the different implementation domains of the customer experience (the brand experience, the interface, and innovation) affect customer equity.

After that, I turn to the bottom part of the model and examine the organizational requirements needed to create and enhance the customer experience. How do these requirements relate to the different aspects of the experience? At the end of the chapter, I look at the employee experience and how it can be a motivator throughout the organization.

Customer Equity: Treating Customers as Financial Assets

Customer equity is defined as "the sum of the total of the discounted lifetime values of all of [the firm's] customers."[1] Customer equity arose as a concept and measurement tool (see Box 9.1) in the late 1990s in response to the need to link marketing and management actions to financial outcomes.

Applying the concept of customer equity, managers can use financial valuation techniques and data about customers to optimize the acquisition, retention, and selling of additional products to a firm's customers throughout the customer life cycle. Doing this involves three steps:

1. Collect relevant customer data (in particular, data about acquisition rates, retention rates, and add-on buying rates).

2. Use these data as well as margin and marketing expenditures to compute four key measures: the customer's *expected acquisition equity, retention equity, add-on selling equity* over a customer's lifetime, and *overall expected customer equity.*

3. Develop acquisition, retention, and add-on selling strategies to maximize the value of customers to the company.

Box 9.1

MEASURING CUSTOMER EQUITY

There are different formulas for measuring customer equity or the "lifetime value of a customer." My colleagues at Columbia Business School, Sunil Gupta and Donald Lehmann, have developed a simple formula that allows you to convert an annual growth margin into an estimate of the lifetime value of the customer. To do that, you need to multiply the margin by a factor they call *margin multiple*. The margin multiple is equal to: $1/(1 + \text{Discount rate} - \text{Retention rate})$. The discount rate is the cost of capital, and the retention rate is the percentage of customers retained over a year (as estimated from market research or the company's customer database).*

Another way of measuring customer equity is by means of the Markov switching matrix, which has been used by marketers for years to model brand switching.[†] In such a model, a customer has a certain probability of being retained at the next purchase occasion. The Markov switching matrix contains the retention probability of all relevant brands (e.g., your own and competitors') and the probability of switching from one brand to any other. Combining the matrix with information about purchase frequency and quantity results in an individual customer's equity and aggregating the result over all customers reveals a firm's total customer equity. To construct the switching matrix is not complicated. However, you need to conduct market research and ask the customer a few simple questions on a regular basis: "Which product did

---

Box 9.1   Continued

you use most recently? What is your probability of buying the following products next time? How often do you use the product? On average, how much do you spend on each purchase occasion?" In addition, information relevant to management such as discount rate, average contribution margin, number of customers and market size, need to be collected or estimated to compute the firm's customer equity.

There are also formulas for measuring aspects of customer equity, such as acquisition, retention, and add-on selling equity. However, the key issue is not just measuring customer equity, but managing and enhancing it through CEM. To do so, you need to model the relationship between customer experience and customer equity. This requires that you construct metrics for each of the three equity drivers (the brand experience, the customer interface, and innovation), and assess them in market research. Then you must link the drivers to the customer equity measure, for example, through a regression model (see Box 9.2).

Finally, the model can be used to project financial impact and the return on investment (ROI) of CEM. Treating the expenditures on improving the drivers of customer equity as capital investments, we can determine whether the improvement in customer equity is profitable by calculating the return on investment to see if it exceeds the cost of capital.

---

*Sunil Gupta and Donald Lehmann, "Untangling the Values of Web Companies." In *Financial Times Mastering Management*, ed. James Pickford (London: Prentice-Hall, 2001, 2.0 ed.), pp. 403–407.
†Roland T. Rust, Valerie A. Zeithalm, and Katherine N. Lemon, *Driving Customer Equity*. New York: The Free Press, 2000.

The concept of customer equity may remind you of *brand equity*. Both ideas propose linkages between the worlds of marketing and finance, and both deal with asset management. However, customer equity is a much more useful concept.

Brand equity is defined as "the assets and liabilities linked to the brand" and is often quantified in terms of name and logo awareness and brand associations. The problem: many of these brand equity measures may track recall, recognition, and image and esteem; but in contrast to customer equity, they do not measure tangible outcomes in customer behavior. Brand theorists have claimed that brand awareness and associations should be related to customer loyalty, higher margins, increased share of wallet, higher levels of customer acquisition, and increased word of mouth. But unless we know precisely *what* aspect of brand equity relates to *what* outcome measure, and how large the effect will be, the concept provides little assurance for top management and investors who are betting their money on strategies to enhance brand equity.

That is one reason the notion of brand equity is receiving increased criticism in the marketing and management fields. It is also being challenged philosophically as a "fundamentally product-centered concept" that offers little insight and guidance for a customer-based strategy:

Viewing customers as assets . . . differs significantly from treating brand equity as the primary marketing asset. The customer asset orientation focuses on a firm's entire future net income stream across brands and services. It does not view the customer only through the narrow aperture of the brand.[2]

As a result, strategies focused on customer equity are more central to many firms than strategies focused on products or brands. Customer equity offers quantification that allows a company to maximize the value that it extracts from customers.

Yet, while customer equity measures are useful for tracking the financial value that customers offer to a firm, they provide little strategic guidance for increasing that value. This is where CEM comes in. It can build customer equity and can specify precisely *which* aspect of the customer experience is likely to impact *which* aspect of customer equity. Thus, CEM can make customer equity an even more useful concept for companies willing to invest in their customers.

Relating the Customer Experience to Customer Equity

According to the CEM model, the brand experience, the customer interface, and innovation are the key drivers of customer equity. Moreover, each implementation domain typically affects a different component of customer equity: the brand experience usually affects customer acquisition; the customer interface affects retention; and innovation is key for add-on selling.

The brand experience affects customer acquisition because it represents the customer's perception of experiential product attributes, the look and feel and the experiential communications, which together amount to a perception of a brand's attractiveness. Customers who find the brand unattractive won't buy it unless they have no choice or price differences are drastic. You are therefore most likely to acquire new customers when you increase the value of the brand experience for them by managing

213

and improving the experiential aspects of the product, the look and feel, and the experiential communications.

The customer interface affects retention because interface exchanges and interactions determine whether customers are satisfied with their relationship with the company and whether they buy again. Thus, the customer interface is generally the most important determinant of customer retention. If you create new value by making the interface easy, convenient, and pleasant for customers, they will give you their repeat business.

Finally, innovation—whether it is a small change, a breakthrough, or a marketing innovation—is critical for add-on selling. Customers are most likely to buy more from a company that they know, but the additional products pitched to them must also be new and innovative.

In many situations, integration is likely to contribute additional value. If done well, it will add to customer equity by improving the perception of the brand, thus attracting more customers at lower acquisition costs than would be possible with poorly integrated brands. Integration will also create more meaningful relations at various interfaces, thus retaining more customers at lower loyalty costs; and finally, it will enhance add-on selling by making new products more meaningful within a product portfolio.

Acquiring customers, retaining them, and selling more goods and services to them over time are imperatives for any business. At any given time, the company must determine whether it has most to gain from concentrating on acquisition, retention, or add-on selling and then allocate resources to the brand, the interface, and innovation, accordingly. For example, research has shown that the high cost of acquiring customers renders many of them unprofitable during the initial years. However, in later years as the cost of serving loyal customers falls, their volume purchases rise and referrals occur, generating big returns. According to some research,[3] an increase in customer retention rates of 5 percent can then increase profits from 25 to 95 percent. Moreover, loyal customers are also more likely to try new offers from the company and thus contribute to add-on selling equity. As a result, over time the company may allocate resources differently to improve the brand experience, the interface, and innovation.

The relationships among the different aspects of the customer experience (the brand, the interface, and innovation) and customer equity are good rules of thumb and generally true. However, if you want precise relationships, you need to establish them *empirically* for your own situation. You can do this by developing metrics for customer equity and for the three experience domains and then relating them and measuring success with an empirical model (see Box 9.2).

In addition to using CEM to manage customer equity, you need to ask what is required organizationally to enhance the experience and, in turn, customer equity. Let's take a look at this issue, illustrated at the bottom of Figure 9.1 at the beginning of this chapter.

Organizational Requirements for CEM

As shown in Figure 9.1, there are four organizational requirements for creating a desirable customer experience: "experiential marketing," "EX for HR," "EX databases," and "corporate

Box 9.2

MEASURING SUCCESS IN EXPERIENCE DOMAINS

To measure success in delivering a desirable customer experience requires developing metrics for each implementation domain of the customer experience: the brand experience, the customer interface, and innovation.

The measurement of the brand experience can be accomplished with scales that assess the quality of experiential features, look and feel and experiential communications. This is usually a verbal assessment (e.g., using Likert scales or semantic differentials). It can be done by experts (product designers, packaging designers, graphic designers, and advertising executives) or, ideally, in a survey with customers. Companies should also include competitors' brand experience or experiential benchmarks from other industries, possibly with the calculation of gap scores.

The measurement of the interface and of innovation can be achieved in a similar way, with experts or customers. For the interface, it is critical to assess all transactions and interactions, and if necessary, to weigh them empirically in importance; for innovation, the assessment may be done for all new products and initiatives going back for a period of three to five years.

Finally, we need to measure integration. This can be done by using a few straightforward integration scales on which we ask customers to rate the degree of coherence and consistency among the company's initiatives in the three experience domains.

Box 9.2   Continued

I have developed customized measures such as the ones just discussed as part of my work with clients. Moreover, the customer experience may be related to customer equity with a simple regression model to measure the effect of individual experience components and integration on customer equity overall. The regression weights will indicate the degree of importance of each experience component and of integration for your business. You can also construct more sophisticated models to examine specific relations (e.g., to what degree the brand experience affects acquisition, retention, and add-on selling equity).

---

creativity." Organizational skills and capabilities in experiential marketing are critical for designing the right brand experience; EX for HR and EX databases are the personnel and technology skills and capabilities for structuring the customer interface; and corporate creativity is a prerequisite for engaging in continuous innovation.

Experiential Marketing

As explained in Chapter 1, traditional marketing is not customer focused. Instead, it has a narrow focus on functional features and benefits of products; it lacks a broad concept of competition and views customers as rational decision makers. Traditional marketing cannot account for the image and imagination qualities that a product provides; it does not acknowledge that customers frequently engage in emotion- and affect-driven purchases; and it has no appropriate methods for researching the customer experience.

To become *oriented to customer experience,* the entire field and institution of marketing must change—the frameworks, concepts, and methodologies, as well as the mind-set of brand and product managers, communication managers, and market researchers. Marketing needs to adopt, as an organizational skill and capability, what I have called *experiential marketing.* I presented the key ideas of this new marketing paradigm in my book *Experiential Marketing* and touched on them in this book. Moreover, the experiential-marketing philosophy provides the basis for the CEM framework.

Experiential marketing focuses on the usage and consumption situation (instead of products), on types of experiences (instead of product features), and on bringing together and integrating the stimuli that customers receive at all touchpoints.

This requires that marketers define the task of marketing—and their own jobs—anew.

To deliver a desirable brand experience, brand, product, and communication managers must not view themselves just as brand stewards, who guard and protect the brand. They are also brand producers, who bring the brand to life at all touchpoints. If you are looking for a metaphor, forget war and the courtroom; instead, think movies and show business! Brand producers should not miss any opportunity to stage an attention-getting and value-creating brand experience.

In a similar way, marketing researchers need to understand that they must employ realistic stimuli in naturalistic situations. The research must adequately represent the situations that customers face when they buy and use goods and services.

Marketing researchers are as much customer anthropologists as they are empirical scientists.

These are not just changes in terminology. They are fundamentally new ways of defining the task of marketing and of reorienting the field toward what really provides value to the customer and the company.

EX for HR

How can we make sure that employees create the desired interface experience whenever they talk to, interact with, and provide information and service to our customers?

Many traditional human resource theories and practices that try to align human behavior with company missions, visions, and values are too abstract and generically focused on broad-based organizational objectives. What we need are customer-focused human resource practices and a step-by-step process for aligning employee behavior to deliver the right experience.

Imagine, for example, that an organization decides to provide clear communications to its customers in all its interfaces. What does this mean for every employee's behavior? How should employees be recruited? How should they be trained?

I have developed "EX for HR" as a methodology to address precisely such questions. EX for HR uses the following five-step human resources process to achieve alignment around the desired interface experience (see Figure 9.2):

1. *Recruiting employees.* When recruiting employees for the customer interface, you need to go beyond just checking

219

step 1 Recruiting employees

step 2 Training for experience delivery

step 3 Providing incentives and rewards

step 4 Measuring behavior against experience standards

step 5 Providing the right employee experience

FIGURE 9.2

The Five CEM Steps for Aligning Employee Behavior

out their resumes. Look at their background and their attitude and assess whether they are likely to go the extra mile to focus on the customer experience. Do they enjoy people? Do they understand the importance of the customer experience? Are they willing to expend the energy to provide a memorable experience for their customers? Do they understand what it means to align their behavior with the customer experience? How do you know? Ask them what they would do in a given situation or have them role-play.

2. *Training for experience delivery.* Once you have recruited employees with experiential skills and attitudes, they need on-the-job training so that they deliver the right experience to customers. Training does not mean simply

teaching employees stock phrases and rehearsing them in prefabricated scripts. Employees should understand the importance of their role and have the freedom to find new ways to enhance the customer experience. You should also encourage them to think from the customer's point of view at all times, no matter what job function they perform. Whether they are selling goods or services, employees should put themselves in the customer's shoes.

3. *Providing incentives and rewards.* Training is usually not enough to ensure that employees maintain customer-centered over time. It is important to provide employees with meaningful incentives and rewards to acknowledge their ongoing customer-centric accomplishments.

4. *Measuring behavior against experience standards.* There is an old management adage: "What gets measured, gets done." Managers must measure desirable employee behavior against a performance standard that focuses on the customer experience. Employees should receive feedback about their performance based on this standard.

5. *Providing employee involvement.* Finally, it is critical to involve employees in interface designs. You need to solicit and incorporate their suggestions about the customer interface so that they give customers the best service possible. In addition, you must find ways to ensure that their work is challenging and personally rewarding. If employees feel bored or oppressed or think that management ignores their input, they are unlikely to deliver a good experience to their customers.

EX Databases

The customer database is another internal requirement for structuring the interface, especially the electronic one. But such databases, especially if customers have access to them (e.g., when checking their bank account, a frequent flyer account, or an online order), need to be experience focused, not just internal accounting tools! They need to be what I call "EX databases."

The little details in a database often tell customers whether a company's priorities are internal operations or customer experiences. For example, can the customer select his or her own password, or does the company assign it? When the company assigns it, can the customer change the password into a meaningful, mnemonic one? Is it easy to select a password, or are there all sorts of complicated rules (at least 8 characters of which at least 2 have to be numbers but no strange characters like hyphens, and so on)? What happens when the customer forgets the password? Is it easy to get a new one—or does it have to be *snail-mailed*? Customers are perceptive about how much thought and care a company has given to their experiences.

Take another example. What information do your front-line employees have available when they interact with customers? Does the information help them serve customers better? Is it up-to-date? Is it up-to-the-millisecond (that is, *real time*)?

Finally, your databases should allow space for storing special information. The database should include information that allows you to celebrate special anniversaries of the customer as a loyalist of the brand. If you are in the airline business, your system should trigger an alert when a customer has taken 50, 100, or 500 international trips with you; and you should do something special to mark those occasions. If you are a phone company, you should send an SMS message for a customer's birthday. That is what an "EX database" is for! The databases should record information that the customer cares about as well as information that your employees can use to service customers. In addition to being an internal record-keeping device for the company, databases must be experience-focused to provide relevant differentiation.

Corporate Creativity

Creativity is about something new, original, and useful. For innovation, corporate creativity is the key organizational requirement. As the internal prerequisite for innovation, corporate creativity can generate anything from a small idea to a radical innovation.

For many years, psychologists have stressed that creativity is not only a free-wheeling, divergent thinking, and brainstorming phenomenon. It is also an attention-guided, convergent thinking, and brain-focusing process. Without this structured phase, creative ideas may be new and original, but they are not really useful. In fact, the creative process often starts with a convergent-thinking, analytical phase that facilitates the later divergent-thinking illumination phase. At the end of the creative process, another structured phase is usually needed to judge how truly original the idea is.

The challenge of an organization is to capture this dual nature of the creative process for innovation. How can managers do this? I have co-authored a book that explains how to do it in detail: *Build Your Own Garage: Blueprints and Tools to Unleash Your Company's Hidden Creativity.*[4] In this book, my co-author and I suggest that a company needs to bring together two seemingly incompatible skills and capabilities: *the bizz* and *the buzz*. Together, the bizz and the buzz assure that innovation can occur. The bizz refers to fundamental management rules; it is about time-tested proven procedures and principles of management action. The buzz, on the other hand, refers to the creation of a motivating climate of excitement, risk taking, and thinking outside-the-box.

Structurally, management needs to make sure to include the bizz and the buzz in any innovation project. You can do this by putting employees from different departments associated with divergent skills, or who are different personality types, into a cross-functional team. You can do it by alternating between bizz and buzz over the course of a project. You can do it by using certain tension resolution tools that we featured in our book (such as Creative Synthesis, Balancing, or Oscillation). No matter what techniques you employ, always think bizz *and* buzz, and not bizz *or* buzz!

Box 9.3 shows how we can measure the organizational requirements for designing the brand experience, structuring the customer interface, and engaging in continuous innovation. Underlying these more specific requirements, however, is a broader organizational requirement that—if done well—infuses

Box 9.3

MEASURING INTERNAL RESOURCES

Just as we developed metrics for measuring customer equity and the customer experience, we can also develop metrics for measuring internal resources and its different aspects. It is just a bit harder.

Because of internal politics, this sort of measurement "behind the scenes" (within the organization) is likely to be less objective and hence less reliable. Ideally, management consultants should provide ratings after they have become familiar with the organization.

For experiential marketing, we interview marketing personnel and record their practices and behavior on a structured scoring sheet. In this way, we can get a good sense of the degree to which marketing is product- versus experience-focused, engaged in piecemeal planning or integrative planning, and so on. You can use a similar procedure for getting measures on "EX for HR," "EX databases," and "corporate creativity."

Once you have developed such metrics, you can relate them to the measures at the other two levels of the model displayed in Figure 9.1—customer experience and customer equity—and test the complete CEM model. Results may be used for allocating future resources, in decision making, and for projecting likely outcomes.

strong motivation through the entire organization: a concern for the experience of the company's employees.

The Employee Experience

In most companies, employees simply do not care about their jobs. According to a Gallup survey based on a random sample of 800 employees, only 25 percent of employees are "actively engaged" in their jobs; the other 75 percent are just muddling through. Dave Ulrich, an HR expert and professor at the School of Business at the University of Michigan, observes that "job depression" is on the rise. Don't expect the job depressed to deliver a great experience to customers. Therefore, it is key for business to foster what Ulrich calls "employee contribution."[5]

Employee contribution becomes a critical business issue because in trying to produce more output with fewer employees, companies have no choice but to try to engage not only the body but the mind and soul of every employee.

How can you engage the mind and soul of every employee? The recommendations of HR experts—empowerment, challenging work, teamwork, communication, fun at work, and so on—are a good start. But managers need to go further.

All these recommendations are specific incentives for better performance; they are focused on the product: work. They are not focused on the customer: the employee.

If employees are *internal customers*, then let's treat them as customers, and let's find out what these customers want. Mihaly Csikszentmihalyi, a professor and former chairman of the Psychology Department at the University of Chicago, has done some fascinating research about what people want from their work. He found that people want to experience work as flow. What is flow? It is the state people achieve when they become so involved in what they are doing that they lose track of time. It is a kind of absorption in the process. Flow is about optimal experiences and enjoyment in life, and the ultimate goal is "turning all life into a unified flow experience."[6] When that happens, work does not feel like work, and the separation of work and leisure becomes meaningless. Work and leisure are one whole—called life.

Now, how can employees get to this state, and how can a company help them to get there? Empowerment, challenging work, teamwork, and so on have a role to play; they are likely to get employees out of job depression, but are they likely to catapult them into the stratosphere of flow? Probably not.

Creating a truly rewarding employee experience is as straightforward as implementing the CEM steps, with employees in the place of customers. In addition to learning about your employees' experiential world to find out what they want, ask them what they would change. Instead of imposing a new regime from the outside, let employees help develop their new work environment.

Not only that, get employees involved—really involved—in the brand. Run internal workshops where employees can discuss the brand and what it means to them. Let them suggest ways that they can live the brand in their day-to-day work and personal lives.

Think about the employee interface. What contacts and interactions are there among the employees and the company?

Where and when do they take place? How could they be improved?

Seek your employees' input about innovation. Companies spend enormous amounts of money on R&D and they should also turn to their own employees for insights about trends and preferences in developing new products. Ask your employees for their ideas and include them in developing innovations.

In short, involve your employees in an internal CEM effort. Integrate your approach to include all the touchpoints among your employees and the company. Work toward building a holistic experiential platform for them and engage them in *sense, feel, think, act,* and *relate.* If you pay attention to your employees' experiences, you will be rewarded with a happier, more productive, more proactive workforce.

Utopia? Yes, sadly, many companies today still operate according to a command-and-control system. Strategy is developed at the top and disseminated to the front lines in an environment of fear. This experience-destroying, military model of the organization fails to recognize the innovative and value-creating forces that a positive employee experience can unleash.

Conclusion

In this chapter, I have discussed the concepts that comprise the complete CEM model. This model addresses three organizational tasks: financial planning in terms of customer equity; allocation of organizational resources (including experiential marketing, EX for HR, EX databases, and corporate creativity); and enhancement of the employee experience discussed. These concepts are useful for managing the customer experience and for linking the experience to tangible outcomes and organizational resources. In conjunction with the CEM framework presented in earlier chapters, the complete CEM model once again shows what is unique about this approach. Like no other marketing and management framework, CEM is analytical and creative; it is about strategy and implementation; and its focus is external and internal.

NOTES

Chapter 1

1. Philip Kotler, *Marketing Management: The Millennium Edition* (Upper Saddle River, NJ: Prentice-Hall, 2000), p. 29.

Chapter 3

1. Horace Miner, "Body Ritual among the Nacirema," *American Anthropologist*, 58, No. 3 (June 1956).
2. Ian MacMillan and Rita McRath, "Discovering New Points of Differentiation," *Harvard Business Review* (July 1997), pp. 131–152.

Chapter 4

1. David Hershkovits, "Designing Man: Calvin Klein Still Pushes Our Buttons." An interview in *Paper* magazine (March 2002), pp. 60–64.

Chapter 5

1. Rem Koolhaas, ed., *Projects for Prada, Part 1* (Milan, Italy: Fondazione Prada).
2. Bernd Schmitt and Alex Simonson, *Marketing Aesthetics: The Strategic Management of Brands, Identity and Image* (New York: Free Press, 1997).

Chapter 6

1. Jill Dyche, *The CRM Handbook* (New York: Addison-Wesley, 2001).

Chapter 7

1. James Brooke, "Japanese Masters Get Closer to the Toilet Nirvana," *New York Times* International Edition (October 8, 2002), p. A4.
2. *Trends in Event Marketing*, Study and White Paper by the George P. Johnson Company (2002), pp. 1–8.
3. Gerry Khermouch with Jeff Green, "Buzz Marketing," *BusinessWeek* (July 30, 2001), p. 50.
4. Emanuel Rosen, *The Anatomy of Buzz* (Garden City, NY: Doubleday, 2000).

Chapter 8

1. Ran Kivetz and Itamar Simonson, "Earning the Right to Indulge," *Journal of Marketing Research*, 39 (May 2002), pp. 155–170.

Chapter 9

1. Ronald T. Rust, Valarie A. Zeithalm, and Katherine N. Lemon, *Driving Customer Equity: How Customer Lifetime Value Is Reshaping Corporate Strategy* (New York: Free Press, 2000), 4.
2. Robert C. Blattberg, Gary Getz, and Jacquelyn S. Thomas, *Customer Equity: Buiding and Managing Relationships as Valuable Assets* (Boston: Harvard Business School Press, 2001), 6.

3. Frederick Reichheld, *The Loyalty Effect* (Cambridge, MA: Harvard Business School Press, 1996).

4. Bernd H. Schmitt and Laura Brown, *Build Your Own Garage: Blueprints and Tools to Unleash Your Company's Hidden Creativity* (New York: Free Press, 2001).

5. Dave Ulrich, *Human Resource Champions* (Boston: Harvard Business School Press, 1997).

6. Mihaly Csikszentmihalyi, *Flow: The Psychology of Optimal Experience* (New York: HarperCollins, 1991).

INDEX